Tourist Cultures

Tourist Cultures: Identity, Place *and* *the* Traveller

Stephen Wearing
Deborah Stevenson
and Tamara Young

Los Angeles | London | New Delhi
Singapore | Washington DC

First published 2010

SAGE Publications Ltd
1 Oliver's Yard
55 City Road
London EC1Y 1SP

SAGE Publications Inc.
2455 Teller Road
Thousand Oaks, California 91320

SAGE Publications India Pvt Ltd
B 1/I 1 Mohan Cooperative Industrial Area
Mathura Road, Post Bag 7
New Delhi 110 044

SAGE Publications Asia-Pacific Pte Ltd
33 Pekin Street #02-01
Far East Square
Singapore 048763

Library of Congress Control Number 2008943327

British Library Cataloguing in Publication data

A catalogue record for this book is available from the British Library

ISBN 978-0-7619-4997-8
ISBN 978-0-7619-4998-5 (pbk)

Typeset by C&M Digitals (P) Ltd, Chennai, India
Printed by CPI Antony Rowe, Chippenham, Wiltshire
Printed on paper from sustainable resources

Mixed Sources
Product group from well-managed forests and other controlled sources
www.fsc.org Cert no. SGS-COC-2953
© 1996 Forest Stewardship Council
FSC

Contents

Acknowledgements

The authors wish to thank a number of people who provided support in the preparation of this book. From SAGE, we thank Publisher Chris Rojek for commissioning the book, Assistant Editor Jai Seaman for her encouragement and patience throughout, and Senior Production Editor Katherine Haw for seeing the book through to publication.

We thank Matthew MacDonald for providing research assistance in the early stages of the project and for editing some of the draft chapters of the book. We are very grateful to Amie Matthews for reading and providing insightful feedback on the manuscript, as well as for her assistance in seeking out references and constructing the bibliography. Thanks also go to Richard Lever for proofreading and editing. Richard's attention to detail and critical and editorial comments on the manuscript were invaluable.

Finally, we acknowledge the support of our colleagues, friends and families who have in various ways made a contribution to this book. In particular, Stephen thanks Betsy Wearing for providing the original inspiration for the book, and is grateful to the School of Leisure, Sport and Tourism at the University of Technology, Sydney for its assistance. Deborah thanks Robyn Bushell for minding the School during her absence and David Rowe, Centre for Cultural Research for advice. Special mention must be made of Professor Wayne McKenna, Executive Dean of the College of Arts at the University of Western Sydney, for providing the assistance needed to complete the manuscript. Tamara thanks Nathaniel Bavinton for his ongoing support and intellectual contribution, Jo Hanley, John Jenkins, Kevin Lyons and Kevin Markwell for their advice and encouragement, and colleagues in the School of Economics, Politics and Tourism at the University of Newcastle.

Introducing the
Cultures of Tourism

People travel for pleasure. They seek to explore and experience new places as well as to return to the familiar and the known. Some tourists are motivated to learn about other people and cultures, while others seek through travel to gain insights into the self. Many, of course, simply wish to take a 'holiday'. Each year, hundreds of millions of people around the world leave their homes for varying periods of time to experience the transience, movement and, perhaps, excitement of 'being away', of 'being there'. Tourism has expanded in recent years in both its scope and significance to become a major social, cultural and economic phenomenon. And yet at the heart of this expansion remain intriguing questions about the cultures of meaning, mobilities and engagement that frame and define the tourist experience and the traveller identity. There is a need, for example, to understand the subjective realities that are the experiences (imagined or otherwise) of the traveller/tourist – to delve into what it is that 'they' are looking for when they travel, be they embarking on a package tour, or immersing themselves in the places, cultures and lifestyles of the ecological or exotic 'Other'. Indeed, the assumption that being a 'tourist' is qualitatively different from being a 'traveller' is one that continues to prevail in both the academic literature and popular imagination.

Nevertheless, it is known that irrespective of how or why someone travels, the traveller/tourist is frequently moved by the landscapes and the people they encounter in the travel space whether near to and/or far from their homes and everyday experiences. It is also known that people seek to record or document their travels and travel encounters in some way – in particular, through photography, in diaries and travelblogs, or via postcards and emails home. Travel and tourism have also long intrigued academics and there is now a considerable body of research into such issues as tourism types and tourist motivations, the nature of the power relationships that exist between travellers, host destinations and the tourism industry, and the consequences of tourism for local environments, economies, societies and cultures. The results of these studies have been revealing but it was not until recently that attention turned to examining the nature of the tourist experience and its formation in the travel space. Indeed, it has only been in recent years that the theoretical tools have been available to delve into the lived complexities of travel and tourism.

To fully understand travel moments and practices it is necessary to consider the experiences, perceptions and activities of the traveller/ tourist in the context of a range of overarching political, social and economic factors which frame contemporary tourism and travel. In other words, travel and tourism must be considered at both the micro and the macro levels. To this end, it is necessary to engage with the insights that have come from a number of different academic disciplines, including sociology, social psychology and geography as well as, most obviously, tourism studies. This is the task undertaken in this book, which seeks to consider many significant bodies of work in the study of tourism in order to contribute to the development of a nuanced and flexible understanding of tourist cultures and to highlight the ways in which different bodies of thought intersect with, rather than oppose, one another. In particular, the book argues that tourist cultures are a complex of relationships that occur with, through, and in space – both real and imagined. The book takes as its starting point the idea of the tourist as *flâneur*, from which to introduce the concept of the *choraster* as the traveller self. The framework is thus expanded from one concerned with a disassociated 'gaze' to emphasize a more engaged set of experiences and imaginings, which incorporate all the senses as well as the imagined-real of the traveller space. The most rudimentary outcome of the book is a contribution to the development of a framework for an understanding of tourism that is subject-centred, and also dynamic and capable of dealing with the complexity of contemporary tourism and tourist cultures.

Understanding Tourism

Tourism is a social and cultural phenomenon that has developed into a significant economic enterprise in cities and regions throughout the world. In both developed and developing countries, tourism is one of the fastest-growing sectors of the economy and a major source of employment and investment. The growth of tourism is evident from World Tourism Organization (WTO) figures that show that world-wide international arrivals increased from 25 million in 1950 to 846 million in 2006 (an average annual growth of 6.5%) with a predicted growth to 1.6 billion in 2020 (WTO, 2007). In 2006, international tourism receipts accounted for US$733 billion, which is approximately 11% of global gross domestic product, and provided approximately 8% of global employment (WTO, 2007).

The significant increase in tourism following the Second World War was largely the result of various economic, technological, social and political changes that occurred in developing countries (Graburn, 1989; Urry, 1990). In particular, the significant growth in international tourism in the postwar period prompted Crick (1989: 310) to describe tourism as 'the largest movement of human populations outside wartime'. Similarly, Butcher suggests that:

> Over the last century and a half the achievement of the [tourism] industry has been nothing less than the democratization of leisure travel, from the few deemed worthy, and wealthy enough to partake, to an everyday activity for the majority in developed societies. (2003: 5)

The most spectacular increase in tourism took place in the last two decades of the twentieth century and has made it a 'quintessential feature of mass consumer culture and modern life' (Britton, 1991: 451; see also Wang, 2000). In affluent nations, the increase in tourism and in the sophistication of the tourism industry has occurred in conjunction with increases in leisure time, disposable income and mobility, technological improvements in communication and transportation, demographic changes, and a shift in the axis of personal identity and meaningful social action from production to consumption (Wearing and Wearing, 2001).

Corresponding with the growth of tourism and the development of a global tourism industry has been increasing scholarly attention in tourism emerging from various disciplinary perspectives. Tourism research and explanations have ranged from micro-social psychological accounts, focused on individual motivations and experiences, to macro-social approaches concerned with the globalization of tourism, which, in part, has occurred as a result of the increasing domination of the market by multinational corporations and the growth in international travel. Jafari (1989) identifies four 'tourism platforms' that dominated the study of tourism in the early stages of its development.

These platforms – labelled 'advocacy', 'cautionary', 'adaptancy' and 'knowledge-based' – have exerted considerable influence over the contemporary tourism research agenda in various conflicting and intersecting ways. The first stage of tourism research (the 'advocacy platform') was evident in earlier studies that viewed tourism as an inherently, and overwhelmingly, positive phenomenon. This positive outlook was adopted and promoted by business interests and national governments, in particular. However, researchers increasingly, and perhaps inevitably (Dann, 2000), began to acknowledge and stress the various negative environmental impacts and socio-cultural consequences of tourism (the 'cautionary platform'). Subsequently, there was the development of more critical tourism studies that explored these negative impacts and resulted in the promotion of alternative forms of tourism ('adaptancy platform'). Critical debates within these three stages of tourism research also led to the emergence of the 'knowledge-based platform ... to fill the intellectual void left by the previous three platforms' (Dann, 2000: 368). This platform is generally considered essential for coherent and sophisticated theoretical and critical debate.

Academic reflections on tourism have thus become increasingly critical and sophisticated with the insights of social science disciplines, including sociology, anthropology, geography, as well as from newer interdisciplinary areas such as cultural studies (Cohen, 1984, 2004; Williams, 1998). Although, as Cohen (2004: 1) notes, the critical and systematic study of tourism from within the social sciences did not really commence until the 1970s and did not receive substantial attention until the 1980s. According to Wang:

> [F]or a long period of intellectual history, travel and movement have not been seen as essential features of the human condition. ... [I]n the Western sociological tradition, travel, tourism and mobility have ... long been treated only as *derisive* characteristics of human beings and society, and usually as economic indicators. ... Even today the sociology of tourism is a marginal branch of sociology, and its relevance is doubted by quite a number of mainstream sociologists. (2000: 1)

Various advances in the study of tourism emerged from 'knowledge-based' analyses which Dann (1996: 6–29) identifies as being focused on 'authenticity', 'strangerhood', 'play' and 'conflict'. The first three perspectives are relatively well-established and accepted frameworks within tourism studies, with the notion of 'tourism as conflict' being a more recent theoretical development. Indeed, the 'cultural turn' that has swept through social science research since the 1980s is also reflected in more recent analyses of tourism situated in the conflict perspective, as evident in discussions of travel texts and discourses. Morgan and Pritchard (1998: 12) suggest that perspectives focused on 'authenticity', 'strangerhood' and 'play' are not adequately grounded in an understanding of the significance of the travel and traveller experience. They argue that there is a need to gain a deeper understanding of the tourism phenomenon by considering the actual experiences of tourists as they travel. Their concern is to 'explain the tourist's reality' (1998: 12), to take into account the lived dimensions of tourism. Morgan and Pritchard further suggest that is necessary to: 'move away from the dominant characteristics of tourism ... to look anew at the subject and at the relationships between those who visit and those who are visited' (1998: 12). Thus tourism comes to be regarded as an 'arena of interaction' which is played out through the tourist's encounters and engagements with the spaces, places and cultures of travelled destinations. A number of other authors have also argued for nuanced approaches to the study of tourism which engage with the subjective and experiential (for example, Desforges, 1998; Harrison, 2003; Hom Cary, 2004; Noy, 2004; West, 2006; White and White, 2004). As Wearing and Wearing state:

> The theorization of tourism ... needs ... not only to recognize the interrelation of the site and the activities provided ... at the tourist destination, but requires a fundamental focus on [the] subjective experience itself. While not being divorced from its sociological contextualization, the involving experience allows for the elaboration upon the role of individual tourists themselves in the active construction of the tourist experience. (2001: 151)

Considering tourism through the lens of experience is central to the approach taken in this book and our exploration of tourist cultures. In their work on the subject, Wearing and Wearing (1996) suggest that a useful starting point for prioritizing the experiences and interactions of tourism is to move from understanding the tourist in terms of the gazing *flâneur*, to imagining the tourist as an interacting *choraster*. While thinking within tourism studies has moved on considerably since that paper was published, it nevertheless made a useful contribution to debates at the time, and thus provides something of a touchstone for many of the ideas we present here. It is, therefore, necessary to revisit some of the central arguments set out by Wearing and Wearing before moving on to explore in some detail the contours of an understanding of tourist cultures through the conceptual lenses of experience and space.

From *Flâneur* to *Choraster*?

Wearing and Wearing (1996) argue that early sociological perspectives of tourism largely reflected the dominant theoretical concerns of the emerging interdisciplinary field and assumed initially (at least) an implicit Anglo-centric, male view of the phenomenon. It is only recently that the importance of differences in class, race, ethnicity, age, sexuality and gender has been acknowledged. For instance, Wearing and Wearing suggest that in the tourism literature some of the initial sociological work was concerned with the tourist *himself* and the part that holidays played in establishing an identity and sense of self that were essentially male. Tourism as a subset of leisure was seen in relation/opposition to the (male) world of work. One of the examples they cite is the work of Cohen and Taylor (1976), who drew on Irving Goffman's concern with the presentation of self in everyday life to argue that holidays are culturally sanctioned escape routes for Western *men*. One of the problems for the modern man, they say, is to establish an identity, a sense of personal individuality in the face of large anomic forces that compose a technological world. Holidays provide a free area, a mental and physical escape from the most immediate reality of the pressures of the technological society. Thus, holidays offer scope for the nurturance and cultivation of identity.

Cohen and Taylor (1976) go on to argue that the tourist uses all aspects of *his* holiday for the manipulation of *his* well-being. We will return to these ideas in the chapters to follow. It is important to note at this point that in the tourism literature, these arguments soon became diverted into a debate about the authenticity or otherwise of tourism and the tourist destination (Cohen, 1988; MacCannell, 1976). In many ways, these developments focused attention on the attractions of the tourist destination and away from tourism as experience (although MacCannell did draw attention to the tourist experience as a means of authenticating the self, see Chapter 2 of this volume). Ultimately, however, such a shift objectified the destination – it became a specific geographical site which was presented to the tourist for 'his' gaze (Urry, 2002). Thus the manner of presentation became all-important and its authenticity or otherwise the focus of analysis, with the objects of the gaze categorized in terms of a set of dualisms – romantic/collective, historical/modern and authentic/unauthentic (Urry, 2002). At the same time, the tourist came to be regarded as something of a *flâneur*. Indeed, according to Urry (2002) the nineteenth-century literary construction of the *flâneur* can perhaps be regarded as a forerunner of the twentieth-century tourist in that both were generally seen to be escaping the everyday world for an ephemeral, fugitive and contingent leisure experience (Stevenson, 2003).

The original *flâneur* was regarded as a new kind of urban dweller who had the time to wander, watch and browse in the public spaces of the emerging modern city (Benjamin, 1973). The *flâneur* was a poet, an artist and a 'stroller'. He has been described as an amateur 'street detective' (Morawski, 1994; Shields, 1994) who moved effortlessly and, seemingly, invisibly through the shopping arcades of Paris. The *flâneur* spent his day simply watching the urban spectacle; observing people and window-shopping (Stevenson, 2003). But in the act of strolling, the *flâneur* did not just observe life but was also engaged in an 'archaeological' process of unearthing the myths and 'collective dreams' of modernity (Frisby, 1986: 224). The *flâneur* was a gentleman who stood wholly outside the production process (Wilson, 1995). He was also away from home and in search of the unfamiliar (Lechte, 1995). All of these characteristics, it has been argued, seem to fit the contemporary tourist – or rather established conceptualizations of the tourist (Urry, 2002).

The *flâneur* was unquestionably male, and *flânerie* was a way of experiencing and occupying space that was available (if not only, then surely predominantly) to men. As Wolff points out: 'There is no question of inventing the *flâneuse*: the essential point is that such a character was rendered impossible by the sexual divisions of the nineteenth century' (1985: 45). Alone, women could occupy public space in the guises of prostitutes, widows, lesbians or murder victims, but the 'respectable' woman 'could not stroll alone in the city' (Wolff, 1985: 41).

> It is this *flâneur*, the *flâneur* as a man of pleasure, as a man who takes visual possession of the city, who has emerged in post-modern feminist discourse as the embodiment of the 'male gaze'. He represents men's visual and voyeuristic mastery over women. According to this view, the *flâneur*'s freedom to wander at will through the city is essentially a masculine freedom. Thus the very idea of the *flâneur* reveals it to be a gendered concept. (Wilson, 1995: 65)

But while the signs and symbols he searched for through his use and observations of space may have been those of the collective, the *flâneur* remained detached from what he observed. He chose not to engage with either the people or the places he visited, thus his way of seeing and being in space was highly idiosyncratic and individualistic – it was not interactive. Moreover, as Wilson (1995: 73) points out, there is also a deep ambivalence towards urban life inherent in 'Benjamin's meditation on the *flâneur*'. It is, she claims, 'a sorrowful engagement with the melancholy of cities', arising 'partly from the enormous unfulfilled promise of the urban spectacle, the consumption, the lure of pleasure and joy which somehow seemed destined to be disappointed' (Wilson, 1995: 73). The *flâneur* then becomes 'a figure of solitude' and anonymity; in the 'labyrinth' he becomes passive and placatory – '[t]he *flâneur* represented not the triumph of masculine power but its attenuation', says Wilson (1995: 74). Moreover, the *flâneur*'s way of seeing is singular in its interpretation; his lens and thus his understanding are unchanging.

When applied to tourism, the tourist-*flâneur* is conceptualized as being at the centre of the phenomenon, observing on his terms. As a result, we are left with very little scope to develop from the idea of the *flâneur* an understanding of tourist cultures that can occur in an interactive experiential space and which is capable of explaining in more than a superficial, egocentric way the interactions and exchanges that occur in that space. Such an observation leads us to suggest that neither the male nor the female tourist will gain more than fleeting satisfaction from destinations dressed up to capture the gaze of the *flâneur*. It is necessary to move away from considering tourism solely in terms of the figure of the *flâneur* to recognize the lived complexity of modern life and to develop a framework for investigating the ways in which tourist cultural identities and histories are constituted and inscribed both in space and on the self. In particular, as is argued below, it becomes necessary to conceptualize the tourist space not as one-dimensional and monolithic, but as many places which are constructed through use, visual consumption, imagination and experience (Stevenson, 2003). The challenge, then, is to envision a more nuanced version of the tourist and the tourism experience – one which is capable of providing the basis for an understanding of lived tourist cultures. To this end, Wearing and Wearing (1996) argue that the idea of the *choraster* is potentially more fruitful than that of the *flâneur*.

As Wearing and Wearing (1996) point out, poststructuralist feminist writers (such as Grosz, 1986, 1995a; Irigaray, 1986, 2004; Lloyd, 1989) charged much theory in the social sciences with being 'phallocentric' – in that it privileged the perspectives and experiences of men over those of women and, indeed, the marginalized. Grosz (1986, 1995a), for example, argues for concerted resistance on the part of feminists to male-dominated knowledges and advocates the utilization of strategies which will allow for the development of women-centred knowledges. She argues that theories which begin from women's view and experience of the world, instead of the assumption that the male experience is universal, may more adequately include not only women but other minority groups as well. Grosz suggests a number of strategies for subverting male domination of knowledge, including the questioning of: an adherence to universal concepts of truth and methods of verifying truth; objectivity; a disembodied, rational, sexually indifferent subject; and the exploration of women's specificity in terms that continue to valorize and privilege the masculine. In its place, she advocates the development of alternative ideas based on women's experiences of the world. She herself employs these strategies in reconceptualizing public space (Grosz, 1986, 1995a). While we must be careful not to replace one form of essentialism with another, Grosz's work provides a useful starting point for developing a way of thinking about tourist cultures in terms of interaction and experience, rather than as objectified activities or sights. It is in establishing a dialogue in the conceptual spaces between what traditionally have been thought of as 'male' ways of seeing and those that Grosz and others regard as being 'feminine' that such a theoretical framework can be developed. Grosz's work on *chora* is useful here in that it may give tourism studies the scope to consider the tourism experience as involving both guests and hosts and the places within which encounters between them occur.

Grosz (1995b: 51) argues that *chora*, Plato's space between being and becoming or the 'space in which place is made possible', contains many of the characteristics which masculinist knowledge has expelled. Rather than being the object of the stroller's gaze, the concept of *chora* suggests a space which is occupied and given meaning by the people who make use of and interact in it, and as such, is open to many possibilities:

> *Chora* then is the space in which place is made possible. ... It is the space that engenders without possessing, that nurtures without requirements of its own, that receives without giving, and that gives without receiving, a space that evades all characterization, including the disconcerting logic of identity, of hierarchy of being, the regulation of order. ... (Grosz, 1995b: 51)

Wearing and Wearing (1996) suggest that, in reappropriating the implied maternal dimensions of space, as Grosz suggests, it is possible to orient the ways in which spatiality is imagined, lived and used, and thus to make way for the silenced/marginalized to reoccupy the places from which they (discursively) have been constrained, re/displaced or expelled. It may also expose men's appropriation of the whole of space. With regard to tourism, they suggest that the concept of *chora* is capable of providing nuanced insights into the tourist experience and opens the way for tourist destinations to be seen and understood as spaces in which people interact with places, peoples and cultures. In turn, the spaces (destinations) as they are lived and experienced take their meaning from the people who occupy them.

Tourism, Experience and Space

Space is deeply implicated in the experiences and processes of travel and tourism. Indeed, tourism is first and foremost about a series of direct and mediated relationships with, and in, the context of space/place (Young, 2009a). The spaces of tourism are the spaces of movement, destination, experience, memory and representation. They are also spaces of desire, fantasy, creativity, liminality, reordering and enchantment. Increasingly, too, tourism is about the spaces of the virtual and the imaginary. By conceptualizing tourism and the tourism experience through a theoretical lens that situates the interactive and enveloping spaces of tourism at the centre of the analysis, it soon becomes evident that there are important and intangible dimensions to space and the spatial structuring of tourism. One of these dimensions is that which can best be described as having been informed by the 'structures of feeling' (Williams, 1961), or the interconnected configurations of meaning, that result from both individual and shared relationships to, and conceptions and experiences of, given spaces, including tourism spaces. Such sentiments also exist at the level of myth, forming networks of understandings, connotations and meanings that are particular to individual cultures (Barthes, 1973). The realization that the tourist space has powerful symbolic dimensions raises a host of related concerns and issues which render partial those analyses that are based solely on narrow, systematic understandings of society, space and tourism.

The idea of the travel space as *chora* suggests that the 'social value' of this space may be of greater analytic value than that of the 'image' associated with the gaze of the tourist *flâneur*. When the term is applied to a place with, and in, which people interact, and to which they attach cultural meanings, it becomes a social process whereby a place acts as a resource that over time has significance for a group of people. Social value, then, refers to the meanings people attach to place. The experiential value derived from the history of a place and its representation sets the scene for its social worth; and its maintenance and the continual interaction of people with it ensure the persistence of this social value. As the social value of a space is a process dependent on there being a dynamic relationship between the place and the people who use it, the meaning may change and develop over time. The people who give social value to the *chora* – the *chorasters* – are those who 'practise' the place, who use it, experience it and give it meaning. These are local residents and service providers, as well as tourists. And the meanings and values which are developed emerge through processes of interaction, negotiation, cooperation and contestation. Gustafson (2001: 5) found the meaning that is attributed to a place 'can be mapped around and between the three poles of self, others and environment', and therefore, the meaning of a place, especially that which residents deem to be 'home', is highly dependent on locals.

The promotion of tourist destinations as 'image' incorporates the fleeting, the ephemeral and the voyeuristic elements of the tourist gaze as well as suggesting a commodified, predetermined mass experience. As Lefebvre observes:

> Leisure spaces are the object of a massive speculation that is not tightly controlled and is often assisted by the state (which builds highways and communications, and which directly or indirectly guarantees the financial operations, etc.). This space is sold, at high prices, to citizens who have been harried out of the town by the boredom and the rat-race. It is reduced to visual attributes, 'holidays', 'exile', 'retreat' and soon loses even these. (1976: 84)

Social value, on the other hand, can incorporate the historical associations which have, over time, been given to a place by the diversity of people who have inhabited it; and it allows for individual tourist experience and the process of social exchange that occurs between the tourist and the host community. Eventually this exchange could become part of the image. Where the 'image' of the place traditionally has been dominant in tourism, we suggest instead a space for 'social value' where the interests and needs of local residents and local communities frame an interactive experience which extends for the tourist beyond that of her/his temporary stay. While it is acknowledged that community participation in tourism development has historically been somewhat problematic and subject to numerous constraints, appropriate approaches that utilize creative, engaging and educational techniques have the potential to be applied (Haywood, 1988; Wearing, 2001). Furthermore, there is evidence that many of the most successful tourist precincts and sites are those that are populated and frequented by local residents (Markwell et al., 2004).

In conceptualizing tourism through a theoretical lens that is grounded in the spaces and selves of the tourist experience, we join other significant contributions to the field (for example, Crouch, 1999, 2000; Edensor, 1998; Rojek and Urry, 1997) to move beyond traditional activity-based analyses of tourism to an approach that is space- and subject-centred. The underpinning premise is that the interactions of the tourist in, and with, the spaces of tourism, and the relationships which tourists form with people and places as part of these interactions, are linked to the construction of the traveller self. Tourist cultures, and thus the traveller self, are multiple and contradictory, constructed and reconstructed through the negotiation of experience that occurs in the context of tourist space. This understanding of tourism assumes that in the first instance tourism is about engagement. Tourism comes to be viewed as a process of expanded social interaction whereby self-identity can be enlarged through the intersection of differing places, peoples, cultures and societies.

In framing this approach, we are operating within a definition of culture which locates the ways of life of a group of people as being intrinsically related to the spaces and places within which they conduct their lived (travel) experiences. Following the work of Henri Lefebvre (1991), culture is understood as being derived from lived experiences and the idea of home and attachment to place is a form of knowledge that is as much practical as discursive. Such forms of knowledge are challenged, modified and even reinforced by the spatial mobility characteristic of contemporary globalization (see, for example, Rojek and Urry, 1997; Sheller and Urry, 2004; Urry, 2000, 2003). Importantly, cultures cannot be thought of as single, delimited and homogeneous units that are simply and unproblematically equated with particular ways of life (Clifford, 1992; Friedman, 1994; Lovell, 1998; Tomlinson, 1999; Welsch, 1999). On the contrary, all cultures 'get remade as a result of the flows of peoples, objects and images across national borders' (Rojek and Urry, 1997: 11). As Sheller and Urry (2004: 3) note, 'almost no countries are not significant senders and receivers of visitors'. It is thus necessary to move also beyond a monolithic singular notion of the existence of an identifiable 'tourist culture' to an understanding that there are multiple tourist cultures which are simultaneously varied, contradictory and overlapping. It is only within such a conception that it becomes possible to advance a nuanced and multilayered understanding of the experiences, places and selves of tourism.

The movement of people and groups, of course, predates tourism. Migrating groups and people bring with them cultural values and practices which are often subsumed or altered by the dominant host populations into which they move (Meethan, 2001). The term 'travelling cultures' was coined by James Clifford (1992) to describe this movement of cultures. He notes that:

> Travellers move about under strong cultural, political and economic compulsions and … certain travellers are materially privileged, others oppressed. These specific circumstances are crucial determinations of the travel at issue – movements in specific colonial, neocolonial, and postcolonial circuits, different Diasporas, borderlands, exiles, detours and returns. Travel, in this view, denotes a range of material, spatial practices that produce knowledges, stories, traditions, comportments, musics, books, diaries and other cultural expressions. (Clifford, 1997: 35)

Rojek and Urry (1997: 1) similarly suggest that travel involves the 'migration' of 'peoples, cultures and objects … [and that it] is now clear that people tour cultures; and that cultures and objects themselves travel'. Our aim is to investigate the contours of an approach to the study of tourism that is capable of considering the interactive and mobile spaces in which tourism occurs, and the variety and forms of the tourism experience and the traveller self that are shaped within and through an engagement with these real and imagined spaces and places.

The Structure of *Tourist Cultures*

Tourist Cultures sets out to frame an approach to understanding tourism that is focused on, and sensitive to, the experiential and the spatial. To this end, various social and spatial theories are explored in the book to unravel and reconstruct the ways in which tourist cultures are imagined. This task was commenced in this introductory chapter, which has flagged some of the key assumptions shaping understandings and explanations of tourism. In particular, the chapter has suggested that the work of Wearing and Wearing on the tourist as *choraster* provides something of a starting point for the task undertaken in this book. The *choraster* becomes the traveller self constituted within the *chora* of the travel space and the travel experience.

The book is divided into two parts each comprising three chapters. Part I, entitled 'Tourist Selves', begins with Chapter 2, which highlights the contribution of a number of foundational works within tourism studies to the understanding of the tourist before moving on to situate the tourist experience at the centre of the analysis. Initially, tourism research was not concerned with the texture of the travel experience or tourist cultures but focused instead on tourism activities which could be classified with reference to an ever increasing number of typologies. Such typologies, not surprisingly, did not explain anything meaningful about tourism as it is formed through the interplay of the predictable and serendipitous encounters with the self and the Other. The insights of Chapter 2 underpin the discussion of Chapter 3, which focuses on some of the key debates in the growing body of literature examining the issue of tourism and identity. This review expands on several themes introduced in Chapters 1 and 2 to examine such issues as the importance of the narrative to constructing the (auto)biography of the traveller self. Chapter 4, the final one in this section, is focused on the Others of tourism – those who are encountered as part of the travel experience and are thus central to the construction of the traveller self. The significant relationships here, of course, are those that develop between the tourist as 'guest' and those who inhabit the visited destination – the 'hosts'. Particularly complex are the host–guest relationships that develop in the context of Western travel to non-Western or 'developing' places.

There is considerable evidence to suggest that host–guest relationships and forms of travel are uneven and often exploitative. But we suggest that this view is overly simplistic and the connection between hosts and guests, the traveller self and Other, is multifaceted and dynamic. Indeed, it takes on a particularly revealing complexion when considered in relation to gender and travel, and specifically to international sex tourism, which is discussed in the chapter with reference to an emerging phenomenon – Western women whose travels to developing countries involve sexual encounters with local men. The selves of tourist cultures are thus shaped by the interplay between the traveller identity, hosts and guests. The chapter concludes by noting the importance of space to the formulation of tourism cultures as experience and the traveller self as *choraster*. These are the issues discussed in the second part of the book, which extends the themes canvassed in Part I to consider the (real and imagined) spaces and places of tourism.

Part II of the book, entitled 'Tourist Spaces', commences with Chapter 5 and is concerned with tourists' interactions with, and experiences of, place and the relationship of space to tourist cultures and the traveller self. By deconstructing the self/Other dichotomy, which positions place as 'the other', it is possible to see that experiencing space through travel can play an important part in extending the boundaries for understanding the traveller self. Our discussion here outlines the importance of space in the tourist experience and in shaping the interactions that occur in the visited places. We suggest that a sustainable approach to tourism might be one where local environments and communities are treated with respect, and where human-to-human and human-to-environment interactions are given priority. In Chapter 6, the intersecting and competing 'forces' of contemporary tourism – the global and the local – are introduced and discussed as the chapter seeks to understand the impact of global tourism on the spaces of the local – the 'Other'. We acknowledge that globalization has the potential to erode local cultures and ways of life, and many tourism destinations risk becoming homogenized as the international tourism industry undermines their social fabric and cultural distinctiveness. The chapter argues, however, that homogeneity is never absolute and that local communities are able to exercise a degree of control over the effects of global tourism on their spaces and cultures. The chapter also considers the activities of the contemporary global wanderer in this process. These travellers – or backpackers (as they are increasingly called) – are often keen to experience the local and the Other and to 'give something back' to the people and places they visit.

Space, of course, is as much about the symbolic and the representational as it is about the physical and the tangible (Stevenson, 2003), and this is true also of tourism space. The task undertaken in Chapter 7, therefore, is to consider the way in which tourist cultures, experiences and identities are constructed through the spaces of the media, image and imagination. The chapter suggests that what is 'real' for the tourist is not necessarily the physical experience or the 'authenticity' of a site, but the impact of the tourism experience on the self – which is often related more (or as much) to the way it is remembered through film, photography and travel writing. In this sense, the tourist creates the 'real' within her/himself in the form of new knowledge acquired through an engagement with the destination. Significant too are the various notions of authenticity, as they have been applied to tourism, and the manner in which the industry seeks to represent tourism destinations. We explore the emerging phenomenon of virtual tourism, as experienced in IMAX theatres and the internet. Important here is the intersection of the real and imagined dimensions of travel and the ways in which new technologies are reshaping what it means to travel and to be a traveller. They are fracturing established notions of the real and the imagined and home and away but we go further than this to suggest that it is now necessary to find a new language for talking about the travel space. To this end, the concept of 'thirdspace' is introduced in an attempt to reconceptualize the configuration of memory and imagination that constructs the spaces and experiences through, and in, which the traveller self is constituted and exposed. Thirdspace is the imagined-real. Finally, the chapter argues that the concept of the thirdspace makes it possible (indeed necessary) to transcend the established dichotomies, such as real/imagined, host/guest, authentic/unauthentic, traveller/tourist, home/away, and self/Other, that continue to be influential within tourism studies. The result, we suggest, is a more nuanced and sophisticated way of understanding contemporary tourist cultures. The concerns of the book thus come full circle and in the final chapter we reiterate the value of an approach to understanding tourist cultures that is multidisciplinary and which places the spaces and interactions of the traveller self at the centre of the endeavour. Significantly, we argue that the key is not in moving conceptually from understanding the tourist as *flâneur* to the notion of the *choraster*. Rather, it is to conceptualize travel and the traveller self simultaneously through the interpretative and sensory 'thirdspace' of both.

PART I

TOURIST SELVES

2

The Tourist Experience

Much of the theorizing about tourism has sought to understand why people travel and to explain the centrality of travel (as a complex set of social and cultural practices) to contemporary society and the contribution it makes to the economies of cities and nations around the world. In particular, different approaches to understanding travel and the tourist experience have recognized that tourism encompasses a diverse range of sometimes contradictory activities and experiences. In this chapter, we trace some of the key developments in seeking to understand tourism in terms of the tourist experience. Our focus is directed first towards the foundational works that have been most relevant and influential, particularly those that situate the tourist as 'subject' at the centre of analysis. We explore the relatively recent shift in conceptualizations of tourism from a primarily consumption-based approach to the view that the tourist is the active creator of his/her travel experience.

In considering the tourism experience, it is necessary to begin by understanding the role that tourism plays in contemporary society, the nature of tourism as consumption, and the political and economic struggles that may be waged over those spaces and experiences that have become particularly valued as commodities. The chapter commences with a discussion of conceptualizations of tourism in terms of typologies of activity which gives a context for understanding the different perspectives that have shaped academic knowledge of tourism and the tourist experience, and which provide the foundations for understanding the traveller self. The chapter concludes by suggesting that an approach to the study of tourism that recognizes the role of subjectivity allows for an exploration of tourists as active creators and producers of the travel experience.

Functions and Formulations

There is still much contention and debate over the meaning of the term tourism (Rowe and Stevenson, 1994), which indicates, in part, that tourism is a field of study that is constantly changing. Indeed, just as tourism is undergoing a range of transformations in scale and type (Fieffer, 1986; Levenstein, 1998; Löfgren, 1999; Meethan, 2001), so too is its definitional theorization (Franklin and Crang, 2001; Hollinshead, 2000). Meethan (2001) proposes that the most obvious of these shifts has been the simultaneous development of mass consumption forms of tourism on the one hand, and of niche and alternative forms of tourism on the other (discussed below). Tourism now encompasses markets located within national boundaries as well as those that are organized on a global scale. Indeed, as is demonstrated in the chapters to follow, the 'placelessness' of the mass tourist experience is increasingly being countered (at least rhetorically) by an emphasis on the identity of place and the local (Stevenson, 2000).

The study of tourism has been the concern of a number of traditional academic disciplines. Nevertheless, it is possible to identify two broad disciplinary approaches or categories of study as significant. First, there is research that has focused on the business of tourism, including tourism management, marketing and policy, which aims in particular to assess (measure) the economic significance (benefits) of tourism on destination cities and regions. These studies generally acknowledge and promote the economic importance of tourism and attempt to quantify its value to host economies and count tourist movements. In this sense, tourism is viewed as an industry – as a business or enterprise that is of economic importance and has significant (positive) outcomes. Second, there is research within humanities and social science disciplines, including sociology, geography and cultural studies, which identifies the limitations of those analyses that emphasize only economic implications and statistical measurement. It is argued that approaches that only consider tourism in terms of economic activity and impact fail to recognize that tourism is a significant social and cultural practice that has considerable positive and negative effects on peoples and places around the world.

The starting point for these often qualitative studies is to accept that economic analyses provide 'crucial information for understanding the phenomenon' but to argue that this knowledge is somewhat limited in that it 'tell[s] us very little about the diverse qualities of tourist experience' (Rojek and Urry, 1997: 2). A social science approach to studying tourism is concerned with providing a broader and more critical understanding of tourism as a social phenomenon. Tourism research from a social and cultural perspective is more concerned with 'conceptualising the forces which impact on tourism and, through an analysis of these forces, providing a broader context for understanding tourism' (Mowforth and Munt, 1998: 3). Needless to say, the approach we take here in considering tourist cultures and experiences is not one that is concerned with economics, marketing and management, although we would argue that approaches to travel and tourism that put the social and cultural first are more likely to produce insights that will lead to tourism that is also economically sustainable.

Wearing argues that it is possible to identify 'two major themes' in sociologically informed studies of travel and the traveller self:

> First, there has been an emphasis on tourism as a means of escape from everyday life, even if such escape is temporary. Secondly, travel has been constructed as a means of self-development, a way to broaden the mind, experience the new and different and return in some way enriched. (2002: 244)

The topic of the tourist experience has been addressed in a number of academic works conducted within social science disciplines since the 1960s (Uriely, 2005), and while much contemporary research regarding the tourist experience corresponds with the so-called post-modern turn in the social sciences and with the postmodernization of society more generally, the majority of tourism studies carried out in the 1960s and 1970s were underpinned by theories which positioned leisure and tourism as being instrumental to the functioning of societies and economies of the West (Wearing and Wearing, 2001).

Early developments in the study of the tourist experience focused on 'identifying and defining the nature of the experience of tourists. ... [T]heorists tended to define these experiences in broad relation, or opposition, to other types of experience' (McCabe, 2005: 88). For instance, some conceptualizations of the tourism experience accentuate 'its distinctiveness from everyday life' (Uriely, 2005: 203). This distinction is evident in definitions of tourism proffered by Cohen (1972, 1979), Graburn (1989), MacCannell (1989), Smith (1989) and Turner and Ash (1975). From this perspective, the tourism space was presented as being distinct in both spatial and symbolic terms – as a place set apart from the world of work, as well as an actual location or destination (Böröcz, 1996; Hall and Page, 1999; MacCannell, 1989, 1992; Urry, 2002; Wang, 2000).

Narrow conceptualizations of tourism that focused on time or activity were in many ways significant factors limiting the development of tourism theory and its ability to address the complexity of the tourist experience. A consumption-based approach to understanding tourism regards the tourist as a subject who consumes products and experiences that have been provided for them by the leisure and tourism industries. According to Cohen (1979), tourism, as an industry in mid-twentieth-century postwar Western society, was regarded as being functional both for the smooth running of society and for the mental and physical health of individuals (particularly workers) within it. In this schema, tourism is regarded as an institution, the chief function of which is escape. But this view also incorporates and reinforces shared social values and assists in integrating various types of action, such as cultural interactions. For example, in the mid-twentieth century (when industry in the West boomed), summer holidays became an important annual ritual for many families in Western countries who typically visited the same holiday resort each year. Holidays at these resorts (invariably located on the coast, by lakes or in the mountains) provided an escape from the stresses and strains of working life. At the same time, holidays at these locations involved participation in a range of activities that were said to promote socialization and reinforce shared cultural values (Bammell and Bammell, 1992; Deegan, 1998).

From a functionalist perspective, tourism and tourism destinations were seen as instruments (among others) that supported the social equilibrium and status quo. Tourism was regarded as good for society as well as a reward for hard work; it was a chance for workers to escape and regenerate so that they would be able to function as active and engaged citizens and be workers who maintained high levels of productivity (Farina, 1980). Tourism was thus seen as reinforcing the norms and values of the society. Specifically, escape from work provided time for activities that generally contributed to the harmony and stability of society as well as providing benefits to individual citizens (Cohen, 1968). This view also reinforced and confirmed established gender roles and the gender division of labour that was prevalent at the time.

Functionalist assumptions concerning tourism as time and activity, therefore, are rigid. They allow for a very limited range of interpretations because of the two-dimensional nature of their constructs. As a result, those studies of tourism that were informed by functionalism were unable to deal with issues of power, conflicts of interests, inequalities of access for communities at destination areas, the experience of tourism, the social construction and meaning of destinations, the control and subordination of various groups through tourism (including host communities), and social justice. They were also unable to examine the fluidity of tourist experiences. One form of explanation of tourism that can be attributed to functionalism is the development of tourist typologies which were designed to classify and categorize tourists into types based on certain tourism characteristics and travel motivations, activities and experiences (for example, Cohen, 1972, 1974, 1979; Crompton, 1979; Dann, 1977; Hamilton-Smith, 1987; Krippendorf, 1987; Pearce, 1982; Plog, 1987; Sharpley, 1994; Smith 1989). In other words, these studies set out to identify the 'types' of tourist that exist, the 'types' of experience that they seek, and to categorize these experiences and traveller 'types'. It is important to outline the contribution of such typologies to contemporary understandings of the tourist experience, particularly in relation to the interactions of tourists with peoples, places and cultures.

Typologies of Experience

The seminal works of the sociologist Erik Cohen (1972, 1974, 1979) provided an initial framework for developing a social theory of tourism and for understanding tourist types. Cohen, according to Urry (2002: 8), challenged the idea of a single tourist gaze, maintaining that 'there is no single tourist as such but a variety of tourist types or modes of tourist experience'. In his early writings on the topic, Cohen (1972) argued that tourism is a manifestation of people's desire to visit other places in order to experience the cultural, social and environmental differences that exist in the world. While some tourists desire the experience of difference or strangeness, this desire is not consistent for all types of tourist, with some desiring and seeking the familiar or, as many have suggested, seeking encounters with difference from within the security of the known and the predictable. Graburn (1983) argues that the search for experiences of difference is dependent on the level of cultural confidence that the individual possesses. Cohen (1972) suggested four tourist types – the organized mass tourist, the individualized mass tourist, the explorer and the drifter. The experiences of tourists were differentiated primarily by the extent of their containment within the 'tourist bubble'. The main distinction Cohen made was that mass tourists are content to enjoy the comforts of 'environmental bubbles' while explorers and drifters wished to immerse themselves in host cultures.

Cohen (1979) later proposed a phenomenological typology of tourist experiences that identified five modes of tourist type, with a quest for pleasure at one end and a quest for meaning at the other. Cohen argued that tourist experiences could be located on a continuum, with a desire for mere pleasure at one end of the spectrum and a search for meaningful experiences at the other. He defined these tourist categories as 'recreational', 'diversionary', 'experiential', 'experimental' and 'existential', and argued that each held different worldviews predicated on a relationship with the 'centre' of their own societies and the centre of 'other' societies (Cohen, 1979). Within this fivefold phenomenology of tourist experiences:

> Tourism is then the leisure/recreational experience par excellence in that it enables a temporary escape from the centre, which nevertheless remains of peripheral significance. Tourism was conceived as a reversal of everyday activities but in itself is devoid of meaning. (McCabe, 2005: 88)

Perhaps recognizing the theoretical limitations inherent in an overly simplified typology of tourists, Cohen (2004: 32) recently noted that the schema he was developing was of 'ideal [tourist] types' and acknowledged the 'fuzzy' nature of tourism as a concept (2004: 9). Significantly, however, Cohen's approach to understanding tourists highlights the diversity and plurality of tourist experiences (Uriely, 2005), and other scholars have added increasingly to his conceptualizations (for example, Hamilton-Smith, 1987; Jiang et al., 2000; Mo et al., 1993; Pearce, 1982; Smith, 1989; Yiannakis and Gibson, 1992).

Indeed, a global industry has developed to satisfy the perceived needs and expectations of tourists and tourism as types. For instance, tourism marketers have sought to 'group tourists together on the basis of their preference for particular vacation experiences in terms of: destinations, activities while on holiday, [and] independent travel vs package holidays' (Swarbrooke and Horner, 1999: 91). Thus, the development of tourist typologies has been useful in assisting marketing strategies and providing a basis for economic measurement and forecasts. The tourist experience is presented as a form of activity which is converted to a typology, where the individual tourist is presented as electing to pursue – in their free time – a particular type of tourism (Lyons, 2003; Weaver, 1998, 2000; Wickens, 2002). However, critics of tourist typologies have asserted that such groupings are overly descriptive, demonstrate an ignorance of certain (often important) market segments, and are the products of author value judgements, methodological flaws and an absence of empirical research (Swarbrooke and Horner, 1999). Tourist typologies have also been found to be based on generalizations that are not sensitive to issues relating to gender or cultural diversity (Chan, 2006; Uriely, 2005). They also neglect the voices and perspectives of the tourist (Wearing and Wearing, 2001; Wickens, 2002). Ultimately, typologies position the tourist experience as being 'shaped by the industry and carried out by passive consumers' (Uriely, 2005: 206). Thus, there is little doubt that the work carried out on typologies is insufficient to provide a sound analysis of tourists and their experiences, and that attempts to understand tourism purely as an activity (or set of activities) that fits a typology creates theoretical problems. Tourist typologies are philosophically based on unfashionable functionalist theories and, although they were very important in putting the study of tourism on the academic agenda, they soon came to be regarded as outdated and culturally specific.

A typology always 'leaves many kinds of tourists outside its scope … each individual trip does not always reflect the innermost needs and aspirations of people … "one's purpose as a traveller varies from one locale to another"' (Suvantola, 2002: 63, as per Riley, 1988: 323). In other words, allocating one tourist to one typology for one trip came to be regarded as problematic. No typology can ever effectively provide the basis for the analysis of tourism experiences since the tourist themselves will move in and out of being a certain type of tourist as they progress through a trip (Lyons, 2005; Steiner and Reisinger, 2006; Uriely et al., 2002). Tourist 'types' do not simply fall into one of several clearly defined and conceptually discrete categories but, rather, take up a position along a continuum dependent on their actual lived experiences, which are themselves a product of the interaction of their desires with the possibilities of the destination. Therefore, a more sophisticated utilization of Cohen's tourist 'types' identifies the characteristics of practices and experiences, rather than the qualities attributed to individuals. Indeed, Cohen (2004) himself has noted that individuals are capable of shifting position along this continuum. Also shifting are the points of recognizable differentiation – under continual pressure from capitalist commodification – that mark various 'types' of tourist experience.

Tourist typologies, while useful initially, are overly simplistic; they are based on stereotypes that 'cannot hope to encompass the complex patterns of behaviour we see in the real world' (Swarbrooke and Horner, 1999: 92). The diversity and plurality of tourist experiences need to be understood within the complex and dynamic phenomenon of tourism:

> As the tour group, the host community and the natural environment, to varying degrees, are interdependent components of any tourist experience, there is a need to move beyond simplistic typologies towards a more analytically flexible conceptualization that allows for the exploration of the assumptions implicit in the 'tourist gaze', the tourist 'destination', the marketing 'image', the 'visit', in suggesting other modes of analysis that may better account for the significant range and diversity of tourist experiences. (Wearing and Wearing, 2001: 151)

While typologies can provide a language for describing/categorizing tourism activities, insufficient elements of the tourism phenomenon are explored if analyses are limited to this approach. In contrast, conceptualizing tourism as experience can incorporate such elements of activity at the same time as going further to introduce and develop a more nuanced understanding of a range of other factors, such as, who can be considered a tourist and what are the limitations placed on the tourist experience by the global nature of contemporary tourism. This is particularly relevant as tourism is now increasingly understood 'as one kind of a cultural discourse of the world ... considered as part of the production and consumption of tourist destinations and attractions' (Suvantola, 2002: 2–3). In other words, focusing attention on the quality of the experience rather than the activity will make it possible to discover more about tourism and what makes travel meaningful to tourists. In a recent review of conceptual advancements in tourist experience research, Uriely identifies four key developments that he describes as:

> [sic] [A] reconsideration of the distinctiveness of tourism from of everyday life experiences; a shift from homogenizing portrayals of the tourist as a general type to pluralizing depictions that capture the multiplicity of the experience; a shifted focus from the displayed objects provided by the industry to the subjective negotiation of meanings as a determinant of the experience; and a movement from contradictory and decisive academic discourse, which conceptualizes the experience in terms of absolute truths, toward relative and complementary interpretations. (2005: 200)

Thus, it came to be regarded as being valuable to establish how and why an activity was chosen in the first place and to understand how the tourist actually experienced the activity and made sense of it in terms of their traveller identity. These are the concerns of Chapter 6, which examines tourist cultures and associated traveller identities in the context of the forms of tourism which have, in many ways, evolved from the tourist desire for authenticity within their travels. It is important, however, first to examine the significance of the notion of authenticity to tourism studies and its explanatory value in providing a way of understanding tourism and the traveller experience.

Authenticities and Alternatives

With the discussion of this book leading us towards a conceptualization of the tourist that places interaction as central to the experience, and the construction of self and identity as its outcome, it is appropriate now to explore authenticity and, in particular, existential authenticity which are at the centre of attempts to understand tourist cultures (Harrison, 2003; Steiner and Reisinger, 2006; Taylor, 2001; Wang, 2000). Wang (1999: 360 and 364) identifies existential authenticity as emanating from those 'activities' that allow tourists 'to keep a distance from, or transcend, daily lives' and to find their 'true selves'. The pursuit of authenticity as a primary motivation of tourists has informed many theoretical discussions, and the notion that tourism is a search for authenticity is one of the most well-known and well-established theoretical debates in the study of tourism. Put very simply, travel is understood as being a relentless search for the 'authentic' – a quest for encounters with the 'real thing' (Mowforth and Munt, 1998: 55). The foundational works on authenticity and tourism are briefly outlined below.

Debates about authenticity in tourism commenced with the writings of Boorstin (1987), who provided one of the first social critiques of mass tourism. Boorstin argued that contemporary tourism had become nothing more than a superficial and trivial activity. He was convinced that certain key aspects of travel (adventure, hardship and struggle) had disappeared and been replaced by the superficial and fabricated simulacra of tourism – an approximation of the 'real'. Boorstin believed that tourists were no more than hedonists unable to experience reality directly, thriving on and finding pleasure only in the inauthentic and, therefore, taking pleasure in contrived experiences, attractions and 'pseudo-events'. According to Boorstin, tourists had become no more than passive onlookers who are either unable or unwilling to experience directly the travel reality:

The tourist is passive; he [sic] expects interesting things to happen to him. He goes 'sight-seeing'. ... He expects everything to be done to him and for him. ... Thus foreign travel ceased to be an activity – an experience, an undertaking – and instead became a commodity. (1987: 85)

In contrast to Boorstin's scathing and somewhat elitist critique of contemporary tourism and tourists as celebrators of the inauthentic, MacCannell (1973, 1989) viewed the tourist as a modern secular pilgrim motivated to travel by a desire to encounter authenticity in other places and cultures. He argued that tourism was a search for an authenticity that could no longer be found or experienced within an alienated modern world (see also Mies, 1993). However, according to MacCannell (1973), this quest is ultimately doomed as it is hindered by locals and by the tourism industry. As a result, tourists are only usually able to access the spaces of 'staged authenticity'. So, although tourists wish to experience the 'real' lives of others in authentic 'back regions', they are usually unable to penetrate and move beyond the 'front' regions.

However, as discussed above, tourism cannot be explained in terms of only one type of motivation or set of activities. Rather, tourism consists of a range of contemporary travel practices and various types of tourist. Cohen (1979) argued that the discussions of authenticity by both Boorstin and MacCannell were limited since both had assumed an homogeneous view of the tourist; they had suggested that all tourists behaved in a similar manner and had similar motivations for travel. Indeed, this limitation was the starting point for Cohen's (1979) argument that there are a range of tourist types, each holding different worldviews predicated on their relationship towards the 'centre' of their own and 'other' societies. Cohen (1979) positioned these travellers along a continuum of tourist types seeking varying degrees of authenticity in their travels. The idea of a universal tourist in search of authenticity was further challenged by Cohen (1988), who argued that while some tourists may be motivated by the desire to escape and to engage with the authentic, this is clearly not the case for all tourists.

These foundational works on tourism and authenticity have continued to influence debates within the sociology of tourism and, over the past forty years or so, have been reformulated and applied to various academic discussions of tourism and the tourist experience. Wang (1999, 2000) recently outlined the theoretical formulation and shifting interpretations of the authenticity perspective within tourism analyses. He contends that explanations of authenticity within tourism studies have been simplified into two separate overarching concerns – the authenticity of tourist experiences and the authenticity of toured objects (Wang, 2000: 48). Wang (1999, 2000) goes on to assert from this, that it is actually possible to identify three dominant and different approaches to understanding authenticity – 'objective', 'constructed' and 'existential', the first two of which he claims are 'object-related' and the third is 'activity-related'.

Using MacCannell's 'staged authenticity' thesis as a point of departure, Wang explores the concept of 'objective' authenticity, which refers to the authenticity of toured objects as being 'original' and, therefore, genuine and authentic. In this light, authenticity is thought to be measurable and definable. This externalized view of the concept leads to the second approach to authenticity as 'constructed', whereby the focus is on tourist perceptions of authenticity and refers to the authenticity that is 'projected onto toured objects' (Wang, 2000: 49). In other words, authenticity is the product of social construction. Tourists are seeking 'signs of authenticity or *symbolic* authenticity' (Wang, 2000: 49) at the same time as objects are constructed to appear authentic through images, stereotypes, expectations and power.

In contrast to these object-related forms of authenticities, Wang also speaks of 'existential authenticity', which is grounded in the tourism experience. In this sense, 'authenticity comprises personal or intersubjective feelings that are activated by the liminal process of tourist behaviors' (Wang, 2000: 49). In other words, the nature of toured objects is comparatively less relevant. Instead, authenticity is a subjectively interpreted and 'existential state of Being' that describes a particular kind of relationship with the self, and in some instances with others (hence the notion of interpersonal authenticity), and which is potentially 'activated' and achieved through tourism activities that are perceived as existing outside the constraints of everyday life (Wang, 2000: 49). Wang (1999) emphasizes existential authenticity because it represents people in the process of self-creation through the construction of personalized narratives; an idea that has much to be recommended here because it makes it possible to suggest that the social, cultural and environmental interaction that the tourist experiences in the tourist space is what contributes most to an enhanced and enlarged sense of the traveller self. Yet, it should be noted that some commentators have questioned whether the search for the 'real' and 'authentic' in travel is motivated by personal or existential fulfilment, or is an expression of the pursuit of cultural capital (Desforges, 1998; Meethan, 2001; Mowforth and Munt, 1998).

Importantly, Wang (2000: 46) points out that 'many tourist motivations or experiences cannot be explained solely in terms of the conventional concept of authenticity'. Similarly, Steiner and Reisinger observe that existential authenticity is conceived 'moment to moment' and that:

> Because existential authenticity is experience-oriented, the existential self is transient, not enduring, and not conforming to a type ... a person is not authentic or inauthentic all the time. There is no authentic self. One can only momentarily be authentic in different situations. Thus, there are no authentic and inauthentic tourists, as much as researchers might like there to be such handy categories. At their most extreme, some tourists might prefer to be authentic most of the time while some prefer being inauthentic most of the time. (2006: 303)

Particular types of tourist interaction and travel activity have been situated as being more authentic than others. Tourism has become increasingly fragmented and numerous niche tourism opportunities and experiences have developed as alternatives to the much criticized mass tourism. For instance, environmental tourism, cultural tourism, adventure tourism and volunteer tourism (to name but a few) are packaged by the tourism industry for consumption by increasingly differentiated market segments (Stevenson, 2000). Each of these alternatives seemingly offers more authentic experiences than those provided by contemporary mass tourism, and has ostensibly developed in ideological opposition to mass tourism (Young, 2008). Cohen (1987: 13) states that the 'idea of alternative tourism has its source in two contemporary ideological preoccupations: one is the countercultural rejection of modern mass consumerism, and the other the concern for the impact of the modern industrial world on Third World societies'. Similarly, Eadington and Smith state that:

> Disillusionment with 'mass' tourism and the many problems it has triggered has led many observers and researchers to criticize vociferously the past methods and directions of tourism development and to offer instead the hope of 'alternative tourism', broadly defined as forms of tourism that are consistent with natural, social, and community values and which allow both hosts and guests to enjoy positive and worthwhile interaction and shared experience. (1992: 3)

The changing desires of tourists, and the emergence of tourism forms that are the antithesis of commercial, mainstream mass tourism, are often theoretically positioned within discussions of postmodernism or globalization (Buhalis, 2001). In the alternative tourist's search for experiences, there is an increased interest in seeking authentic cultural contact as well as achieving existential authenticity (Young, 2008). Butcher notes that (what he terms) the new tourist:

> seeks selfhood through experiencing other cultures. ... The new [or alternative] tourist is often seen as intent on gaining an understanding of the host society's culture, and through this, discovering something about themselves. (2000: 45)

Self-development through tourism and an interest in lifelong educational pursuits have become increasingly powerful motivators of travel experiences and have resulted in an increased interest in, and provision of, educational tourism experiences, including ecotourism, cultural tourism and heritage tourism. Cultural tourism, for instance, has been an identifiable sector of the international tourism industry since the 1970s. It is a specific form of alternative tourism that has cultural sites, events and experiences as its primary focus (Stevenson, 2000), with tourist experiences based in 'contact between visitors and locals through experiencing local customs and ways of life' (Craik, 1998: 125). Craik (1997: 119) suggests that a 'broad comparison' can be made between the Grand Tour – that is, the view of travel as educational and enlightening – and modern cultural tourism. She notes:

> By returning to the quest for educational, authentic, experiential and communicative aspects of tourist encounters, advocates and the industry are positioning culture as a central part of the phenomenon. In one sense, this is a return to the primary motivations of the Grand Tour ... it taps into the desire for alternative, special interest and off-the-beaten-track kinds of travel experiences. (Craik, 2001: 104)

Cultural tourism can no longer be considered a 'niche' or 'special-interest' form of tourism and is better understood as an 'umbrella term for a range of tourism typologies and diverse activities which have a cultural focus' (Smith, 2003: 29). Cultural tourists actively seek personal, 'authentic' and 'sincere' experiences in destinations and their interactions with host cultures and communities (Harrison, 2003; Taylor, 2001). According to Smith (2003: 35), 'most cultural tourists are likely to be on some kind of quest for authenticity, either in terms of self-improvement or in terms of the sites, communities and activities that they engage with or in'. The experiences, activities and desires of tourists in relation to seeking cultural interaction indicate that the travel experience is about more than merely sightseeing – it is about participating, experiencing and learning. As Stevenson observes:

> Most commentators agree that cultural tourism is not just about looking; rather, it is about participation and experience … this means coming into contact with what is perceived (or packaged) as 'authentic' in order to learn about a culture or a particular set of cultural practices or productions through the encounter. (2000: 130)

The experiential perspective evident in the above description of cultural tourism underpins our reconceptualization of tourism. The threads of an interactive person-centred approach are being woven together to emphasize the importance of encounters – personal, social, cultural and environmental – in the tourist experience, as well as the significance of participation and learning. Clearly, 'attention' has 'shifted from the displayed objects provided by the industry to the tourist subjective negotiation of meanings as a determinant of the experience' (Uriely, 2005: 206). To be a tourist is to find experiences that are based on being mobile and transient and involved, even if only superficially, in spaces, places and the lived worlds of others (Crouch, 2000; Hall, 2004; Jack and Phipps, 2005; Meethan, 2003). This experience is based on the idea of 'travelling cultures' to describe how tourists move; following others, this term is used here to explain tourist cultures as created and shaped by travel (Clifford, 1992, 1997; Friedman, 1994; Robertson et al., 1994; Rojek and Urry, 1997).

The focus on tourist cultures as being created and shaped by travel and mobility takes us back to our central premise: that tourism experiences are complex, and that tourism is a multidimensional experience. As discussed in Chapter 1, the focus on the gaze of the *flâneur* can be seen as a partial view of tourism, while conceptualizing the tourist as *choraster* provides a more open framework for engaging with the complexity and serendipity of the travel experience. Moving away from an understanding of tourism based on typology or activity to one that foregrounds experience, makes it possible to come up with a conceptualization of tourist cultures that is dynamic. As we explore in Chapter 4, traditional notions of tourism are too limited and inflexible to explain tourism from an experiential perspective, and they do not provide a comprehensive understanding of the complex relationships that exist between hosts and guests in the travel space. Conceptualizing tourist cultures as dynamic involves a view that both control and freedom are integral to the tourism experience. This argument is similar to that raised by Wang (2000) in his discussion of *eros* and *logos*, and the recent work of Matthews (2008b, forthcoming) in her discussion of authenticity and freedom and the ways by which they structure the tourism experience.

The challenge here is to find a language for talking about the tourist experience that accounts for the various social, cultural and spatial spheres within which it occurs. Tourism as time and type is an objective perspective, whereas tourism as an attitude is subjective. Increasingly, tourism researchers are arguing for a more person- or subject-oriented view of the tourist and tourist experiences. Thus, we see various concepts and metaphors drawn on to discuss the tourist experience, including performance (Edensor, 1998), encounter (Crouch, 1999), embodiment (Crouch, 2000) and mobility (Urry, 2000). Central to these developments is a 'strong interest in *the subject* and in what people themselves make of their lives' (Crouch, 2000: 63). The practice of tourism is multi-sensory (Crouch, 1999; Dann and Jacobson, 2003), and it demands 'new metaphors based more on "being, doing, touching *and* seeing" rather than just "seeing"' (Cloke and Perkins, 1998: 189). Indeed, the tourism experience is 'not only an occular one, but truly corporeal … the embodiment of the tourist experience [is] strong and palpable' (Markwell, 2001: 55).

Some authors argue that the relatively recent shifts in thinking about the tourist experience – from simplified and reductionist typologies to more nuanced understandings of the complexity of tourist experiences – are underpinned by postmodernist thought (for example, Jack and Phipps, 2005; McCabe, 2005; Uriely, 2005). The breaking down of tourism typologies, the acknowledgment that tourists are not passive consumers, the focus on existential authenticity, and the recognition that tourism is a multi-sensory and embodied experience are, in many ways, evidence of the shift to a person-centred approach to understanding the tourist experience. According to McCabe: 'Postmodernists emphasize subjective and negotiated characteristics over more reductionist and rigid notions, tending to focus more deeply on the nature of tourist roles, experiences, meanings and attitudes' (2005: 91).

The emphasis on tourism as consumption, discussed above, means that the tourist experience has often been evaluated with reference to their consumption of signs, products and event travel itself (Wearing and

Wearing, 2001). This narrow view of tourist-as-consumer emerged as a result of the commodification processes that occurred as a consequence of globalization and mass consumption (Paterson, 2006). The tourism industry is increasingly structured, with creators of tourist spaces attempting to pre-programme a common tourist experience (Edensor, 2001). However, according to Crouch (1999: 6), while '[p]eople may consume … they make their own sense and value, their own knowledge, albeit negotiated with a myriad of influences'. Such influences may include encounters with other people, material objects, imagination, emotions, memory and space (Crouch, 2001). The focus here is on the tourist as an individual rather than the travel experience as a whole, and suggests that no two experiences are alike because tourists value, use and negotiate space in different ways. Thus, tourism should be viewed as an interactive space in which tourist experiences involve both hosts and guests and the spaces and places within which these encounters occur.

Conclusion

A profusion of tourist experiences have been identified and categorized for the purposes of theorizing, analysing and marketing the products and experiences of tourism. Many authors have proposed typologies based on the nature of the tourist activity and/or the characteristics, motivations and behaviour of the tourists. Yet as conceptualizations of tourism have changed, and with the development of more sophisticated analytical lenses, the raft of tourism typologies that often masquerade as tourism theory have been broken down in favour of more nuanced conceptualizations. In particular, it is now widely accepted that the typological approach to tourism fails to address a range of important social, cultural and environmental considerations. These neglected issues include a lack of acknowledgement of the existence of power differences within tourism, conflicts of interest, and inequalities of access for many communities at destination areas. Also ignored are the experience of the tourist, the social construction and meaning of destinations, and the control and subordination of various groups through the processes of tourism. It was argued in this chapter that conceptualizations of authenticity, in particular those focused on existential authenticity, provide an important starting point for developing a more nuanced analysis.

The recent shift towards more critical approaches to tourism in late (or post-) modernity has promoted increasing recognition of the individualized and subjective nature of the tourist experience. Such conceptualizations recognize tourism as a source of meaning around which many individual lives are being structured. Tourism interactions and serendipitous encounters play a significant role in the construction of the traveller self; indeed, the tourist experience is marked by serendipity (Hom Cary, 2004). The idea of tourism as an experience is presented in this chapter as the starting point for a broader understanding of tourism. Such an approach makes it possible to consider both the limitations and freedoms inherent in tourism and the interactive tourism space. This conceptualization underpins our original discussion of the *flâneur* and *choraster* in Chapter 1. An understanding of tourism in these terms requires an engagement with the ways in which identity frames, and is framed by, the travel experience. It is to an examination of these issues that our attention will now turn.

3

Tourism and Identity

A significant proportion of the early research into tourism was concerned with categorizing tourists and tourist activities and producing typologies that represented tourists. In this context, some interest was directed to the part that holidays play in establishing a sense of self-identity (Bammell and Bammell, 1992; Cohen and Taylor, 1976; Löfgren, 1999). Also important is the notion of authenticity which became a touchstone for sociological explanations of tourism and the tourist experience. In moving away from a concern with typologies and to some extent with authenticity, this chapter explores the ways in which a focus on the tourist self and identity can provide a conceptual framework for understanding tourist cultures and the experiences which shape the traveller. The starting point is to reject the suggestion that tourism is merely an escape from work and to propose instead a more integrated conceptualization that allows for a nuanced understanding of the tourist experience.

The chapter begins with a consideration of leisure in contemporary society and the work–leisure binary that has historically underpinned tourism studies. Here greater emphasis is placed on work in the formation of identity, and leisure is constructed as a voluntary yet commodified distraction. We then chart the growing concern with the notion of identity. This approach provides a conceptual foundation for theorizing the traveller self and tourist cultures that acknowledges a wide range of tourist experiences and encounters. Tourism is thus understood as a process of expanded social interaction whereby self-identity has the potential for enlargement and growth through the engagement of the tourist with other environments, peoples, societies and cultures.

Time to Escape

With industrialization and increasing commodification came the desire for escape and distraction. Thompson (1967), in his classic work on time, suggests that prior to industrialization in the West, time was not experienced as a constraint outside the self which structured life in a fixed and inflexible way. Rather, it was deeply connected to the rhythms of everyday life. But with industrialization, the advent of more precise clocks and the emergence of the factory system of production, there came a type of labour discipline which was based on the regimentation of time. Time was 'administratively' managed (through such things as time-sheets, overtime, time-keeping, time off), with the employer's time and the worker's time being differentiated. For the entrepreneur, time became a vital ingredient in the production process, so much so that 'time became money', and a prime resource to be manipulated, used and sold if necessary. A working day lost came to be seen as a day's pay lost.

Despite some continuity in values and leisure practices from the pre-industrial to the industrial age, leisure activities have come to be constrained by commodified time (Rojek, 1985, 1995). The worker is obliged to pay for the retrieval of time and resources in order to enjoy the benefits of leisure (Brown et al., 2001; Kielbasiewicz-Drozdowska, 2005). Mugford (1987) develops this argument by linking commodified time to Eliade's (1960) ideas of 'desacralized time' and the 'fall into time' of 'modern man'. Eliade (1960) claims that in traditional societies all responsible action, such as labour, handicrafts, war and love, impart a sacramental aspect to human existence, or indeed are sacraments, and so took place in sacred time. This sacred time opened out into 'Great Time' or timelessness. Eliade (1960: 37) says 'the true "fall-into-time" begins with the secularization of work', and 'it is only in modern societies that man [sic] feels himself to be the prisoner of his daily work, in which he can never escape from Time'. Leisure then becomes an attempt to escape from the tyranny of time through a 'bewildering number of distractions' (Eliade, 1960: 37). In capitalist societies these distractions are linked to the commodification of leisure. The blandness and boredom of the transitory and the fleeting – which are characteristics of modernity – pervade leisure as they pervade all aspects of capitalist society (Everingham, 2002; Mugford, 1987: 7). Leisure time, then, is neither 'free' nor 'self-enhancing', but a form of escapism from the equal units of unending sameness that make up commodified time.

Sociological analysis generally, and Marxian paradigms in particular, have tended to emphasize paid labour over leisure – often
referred to as the 'productivist' bias – as a central source of identity
in industrial capitalism (Aldridge, 2003; Fevre, 2003; Giddens,
2006; Grint, 2005; Rojek, 1985). Occupation, paid labour and
employment have been seen, both theoretically and empirically, as
either contributing to an individual's sense of self and self-esteem or
alienating 'him' from a true sense of who 'he' is by divorcing the
product of 'his' labour from 'his' experience. At best, occupation,
paid labour and employment are considered to determine individual
and family lifestyles and life chances in a consumer society. Feminist
philosophers have been critical of the male bias in such analyses, but
many also retain the emphasis on labour as the crucial element for
understanding social position, action, status and social identity by
emphasizing the labour aspect of childcare and household tasks
(Hochschild, 1997; Nordenmark, 2004; Shelton and Firestone,
1989).

In contemporary (post)industrial society, leisure and tourism experiences are being increasingly acknowledged as sites for the construction of individual identity, in addition to identity formation in the
workplace (Rojek, 2005). Moorhouse (1983) argues that such a shift
in emphasis is necessary in order to take into account everyday experiences as significant in the construction of one's identity, or more
precisely identities. The intellectual problems associated with dis-
covering how people construct an identity, including the process of
self-evaluation and the experience of social relationships, are not to
be answered by reducing life to occupation, paid labour and employment, however plausible this may once have been. For most people,
and by no means only those in objectively routinized work, the 'real'
part of life is very often experienced outside paid labour. But more
significantly, there is now a general acceptance that it is not possible
to speak of people as having a single, consistent identity. Rather,
identity is shifting, multiple and decentred. Identity does not have an
'essence' but is fluid and people engage with the world through a
range of (sometimes contradictory) subject positions (Bauman,
2000; S. Hall, 1996). Gender, race, ethnicity, class and sexuality are
central elements of this process, but so too are practices such as
work, leisure and tourism.

A concentration on work alone will tell us very little about most
people's hopes, fears, desires and dreams; or about who people think
they are and how they relate to others. For many people, work is an
annoying irrelevance; their dream is usually to be free of its

constraints. Expression of these sentiments can be seen in the phenomenon of downshifting or voluntary simplicity that has been on the increase in the United States, the United Kingdom and Australia over the last twenty or so years (de Graff, 2003; Drake, 2001; Hamilton and Mail, 2003; Schor, 1999). For some, these social trends represent a challenge to the dominant upwardly mobile ethic of neoliberal societies, represented by employment promotions, increased responsibilities, increased salaries and greater access to consumer items and experiences. Instead, the downshifters opt for a life of greater simplicity by taking less demanding employment (fewer responsibilities, a drop in salary, and a decrease in time commitment), which gives them more time for leisure and family, as well a concomitant reduction in the consumption of goods and services, alleviating the complexity and stress of everyday life. In a recent study of the phenomenon of downshifting in Australia, Hamilton and Mail (2003) found that 23% of respondents had downshifted in the last ten years. The reasons cited for this change in employment arrangements included spending more time with family, a desire for a healthier lifestyle, and greater personal fulfilment.

The shift in emphasis towards leisure has been occurring at political and educational levels since the Second World War. It came about as a result of the institutionalization of the welfare state in many OECD countries (van der Poel, 2006), along with increases in unemployment, early retirement, automation and a reduction in working hours – all of which have been reflected in sociological explanations of the importance of leisure in people's lives (de Grazia, 1964; Dumazedier, 1967; Godbey and Robinson, 1997; Jenkins and Sherman, 1979; Kando, 1980; Larrabee and Meyersohn, 1958). The theoretical underpinnings of the explanations, however, remain for the most part firmly tied to a concept of work as the centre. Leisure continues to be often peripheral to an understanding of individual identity, status, mobility and lifestyle (Fevre, 2003; Rojek, 1985). This has certainly been the model of leisure attached to theories of modernity (Rojek et al., 2006: 4).

From a more practical perspective, empirical evidence indicates that true leisure (in the classical sense) has become subsumed under a 'work and spend treadmill' (Cross, 1993; T. Robinson, 2006; Schor, 1991). Nevertheless, leisure experiences can and do contribute significantly to identity formation, but the relationship is complex. The way people recreate is strongly influenced by the social groups to which they belong – family, tribe, class, associations, communities, nations – and the principles, cultures and laws transmitted through discourse by these groupings (Bhattacharya, 2006; Critcher, 2006; Garton et al., 2004). Some of these influences are easily observed, others are not. Many are so intricately woven into everyday lives that they are almost indiscernible as factors shaping behaviour. For instance, prevailing social attitudes play a role in determining how a person participates in leisure. Many of these attitudes and beliefs are restrictive and reduce the range and number of leisure opportunities available to certain groups and individuals (Darcy, 2007; Deem, 1986; Frederick and Shaw, 1995; Hall and Page, 2002; Jackson, 2005; Pritchard and Morgan, 2000; Pritchard et al., 2000; Shinew et al., 2004). The majority are not founded on evidence; often they are little more than prejudices, myths or social constructions that have been perpetuated over a long period of time, gaining status and becoming part of a society's cultural heritage. Gender is an obvious example, with the discourse on appropriate gender behaviour in contemporary society often limiting women's leisure to indoor, home and family-related activities, and men's leisure to competitive time-related sporting involvement (Wearing, 1998).

In contrast to the macro-social approaches to leisure described above, 'interactionists' turned their attention to the micro-social milieu of individual actors (Atkinson and Housley, 2003). The structures of power in wider society, such as class and gender, were not seen as deterministic within this framework. Theorists in the field of leisure, such as Kelly (1983, 1987, 1994), who drew on the classic work of Mead (1934), focused on the experiential aspects of leisure and on individuals as thinking actors (or subjects) with the ability to construct experiences beyond the ideas of 'escape from'. The suggestion was that styles of leisure (and by extension tourism) are not just combinations of activities, but are also the stages on which we present ourselves and receive feedback on our identities and the roles we play in the social world (Kelly, 1983: 93). Tourism, then, can be said to provide a social space for expression and role reinforcement, as well as being a space for learning new roles, 'playing' with role identities and for developing individual identities apart from those associated with the family and/or work. There is in tourism the possibility, as Kelly (1983: 94) says of leisure, 'to be and *become* ourselves', to develop 'multidimensional ... personal identities' in the ongoing process of 'becoming' (see also Csikszentmihalyi, 1990).

Much tourism can be construed as both personal and social in meaning. Tourists present themselves in a particular role, assuming or establishing an identity. Tourists engage in the experience of travel and the associated role enactment enhances their concept of self in the process. Some roles are quite central to this process and others peripheral; some pervade many social settings and episodes, and others are quite discrete and transitory. Creating the portrayal of a role identity, however, has its own satisfaction at the moment and in the building of selfhood (Kelly, 1983). Identity, then, is the link, through roles, between the personal and the social in a process which develops and changes across the life course, a process in which leisure plays a significant part (Kelly, 1983; see also Rojek, 2005). Kelly (1987) further develops this idea to illustrate how leisure is a dialectic between the actor and her/his environment, with the possibility always of the freedom and choice to create the 'not yet', the freedom 'to become', to expand and develop the self and identity in new ways (Kelly, 1987: 227). Holidays, if conceptualized similarly, thus offer more than a mental and physical escape from the immediacy of the multiplicity of impinging pressures in technological society. They also provide scope for the nurturing of identity. As Cohen and Taylor (1976) have argued, overseas holidays are structurally similar to leisure because one of their chief purposes is identity establishment and the cultivation of consciousness. The tourist, they claim, uses all aspects of the holiday for the manipulation of well-being. This identity is provisional and contingent. It is the identity of the traveller self which is framed and constituted through a particular engagement with the travel process and the places and peoples encountered through the travel experience.

Identity and the Traveller Self

Many social theorists have suggested that the overriding compulsion which governs the actions and attitudes of individuals is the pursuit of a desired identity (Bauman, 2000; Giddens, 1991; Glasser, 1972). In earlier times, an ideal culturally constructed identity was disseminated and facilitated by religious observances reinforced by magic and association with the forces of nature. The pursuit of a desired identity in modern times, however, has been channelled into consumption through the promulgation of an ideal consumer whose main 'freely chosen' leisure activity is to consume. Of course, such an ideal (as constructed by the advertising industry) can never be achieved. Leisure may become something of a tranquillizer, attempting to alleviate the stresses of life. However, the individual is left with a search for identity and a seemingly endless desire to consume. Glasser (1972: 43) adds that 'while the high priests of old aimed at an unchanging model of an ideal identity', the new high priesthood aims to mould an 'ideal consumer', one who willingly makes the changes in lifestyle demanded by competing advertising messages, accepting the idea that anxiety can be assuaged by buying new and more products, 'imagining that each piece of emotional comfort so obtained will be long lasting'. Similarly, Hamilton argues that people are becoming more willing to transform themselves into consumers through their leisure time:

> When consumers are at the point of making a purchase they are subliminally asking themselves two questions: Who am I? Who do I want to be? These questions of meaning and identity are the most profound questions humans can pose, yet today they are expressed in the lines of a car and the shape of a soft-drink bottle. (2003: 82)

In the seminal work of Erikson (1963, 1971), identity is described as a process located both within the core of the individual and in the core of his/her communal culture. These locations give meaning and continuity to individual existence, so that the person can say, 'this is the real me'. Erikson's concept of identity, as a process incorporating something from within as well as from without, restores some balance to the overly deterministic view of structuralists and poststructuralists (Giddens, 1987). One of Erikson's main (1975) contributions to identity theory was to emphasize the importance of understanding an individual's life history or life story, a technique he entitled 'psychohistory'. Viewing self-identity as a narrative acknowledges the cultural and social structures expressed in language and culture, and the individual's desire for personal agency.

Erikson (1963) links identity with play in both childhood and adulthood. By play he means 'freely chosen, self-enhancing experience'. In other words, non-compulsory, non-work, non-production of commodities; a stepping-out of the confines of our normal time and space, social reality and its associated experiences (Wearing and Wearing, 1988). Erikson (1963: 213) adds that 'to the working adult, play is re-creation. It permits a periodical stepping out from those forms of defined limitation which are his social reality.' Erikson is suggesting here that play is an expression of transcendence of the fundamental conditions of existence (see also Turner, 1982). He argues, for example, that play allows individuals to seemingly overcome gravity ('play here gives a sense of divine leeway' and 'excess space'), time (play in its purist form gives no concessions to time), fate and causality (play affords greater control and manipulation), and social reality (in play we step out of our pre-defined roles and scripts) (Erikson, 1963: 213). Erikson (1963: 214) argues that only within these limitations of existence, then, 'can man [*sic*] feel at one with his ego; no wonder he feels "only human when he plays"'. The importance of play and its offer of transcendence provides critical domain for identity formation, self-esteem and self-concept, particularly as they relate to play in leisure and tourism.

Structuralist and many poststructuralist philosophies offer a view of identity which diminishes the relative importance of agency. To ignore that aspect of identity which Mead (1934) terms the 'I' is to underestimate the individual's own experience of personal agency. In his pioneering work on the topic, Mead suggests that identity comes from the synthesis of the 'I' and the incoming information from 'significant others', 'reference groups' and the 'generalized other' of modern society. For Mead, the individual need not and, in fact, cannot be totally controlled by the internalized attitudes of others or the norms and values of society – by the 'me' part of the self. The individual is also an 'I', that is, someone who takes account of the 'me' but is not necessarily determined by it. The 'I' may act upon, influence and modify the social process that it is constantly exposed to. It represents the self in so far as it is free and has initiative, novelty and uniqueness. An individual's various 'selves', constructed in different situations, are not only seen by her/him as discrete objects, but may be perceived all at once in a hierarchy according to the degree of positive attitude that is held towards them.

This perception that the individual holds as a whole person Mead called the 'I' or self-conception. Essentially for Mead, the 'self' is formulated socially and varies with each situation, but it is the thinking person who does the constructing and integrates society into the individual identity. Thus, he claims that the creative artist, the innovative scientist or the charismatic leader can synthesize societal input in new and original ways with the possibility of bringing about changes both in the immediate milieu and in wider society, rather than merely reacting to it. Mead claims that:

> One difference between primitive human society and civilized human society is that in primitive human society the individual self is much more completely determined, with regard to his [sic] thinking and his [sic] behaviour, by the general pattern of the organized social activity carried on by the particular social group to which he [sic] belongs, than he [sic] is in civilized human society. (1934: 221)

In contemporary society there is more opportunity to construct individual identity due to the variety of groups from which to choose. Simmel (1936) also pointed out that in complex industrial societies, the very variety of groups to which one may belong produces a unique pattern of affiliations for each person that contributes to individuality. This observation suggests, then, some possibility of transformation and change, and some hope for individual identity rather than a complete subjective identification with the structural norms of class, gender, age and ethnicity. In Mead's conception, agency is acknowledged, along with the contradictory nature of discourses to which individuals are exposed according to their group affiliations. Mead's work is a significant precursor to the tourism as interaction framework.

The society in which Mead was interested when he questioned how society gets into and becomes part of the self, was composed of significant and generalized others, but these others were most probably restricted to those most similar, in terms of class, ethnicity, race, culture and language, to oneself. Today there is more opportunity, backed up by changes in conceptualizations of ethics and rights, as well as geographic mobility, to experience interactions in tourist spaces which incorporate into self-conception people from different races and cultures in a productive way. Interactionist theories have value, therefore, for developing an understanding of how individuals experience tourism in interaction with the people and symbols encountered in, and through, the tourist space.

More recently, Giddens (1991, 2006), building on Mead's conceptions, theorized what he termed a 'socially reflexive self'. According to Giddens (1991), self-identity has become a reflexive 'project' where the onus is on the individual consciously to select experiences that will contribute to the formulation of an identity in keeping with her/his self-conception. He argues that in an information age the process of social reflexivity has dramatically increased due to the compression of time, space and information. Increases in information, people, products and ideas constantly challenge the way people think about, and reflect upon, their lives. Part of this increase in social reflexivity can be attributed also to the growth in tourism, where multiple interactions and movement in time and space increase interactions between people, places, ideas and information.

For the theorists of late modernity, individualization and the dissolution of stable and enduring structures are indicative of a transition into a more fluid and, thus, unstable social milieu. While aspects of this transition can be celebrated as the liberation from rigid and determining structures dictating life chances, the key significance of late modern 'liquidity' is predominantly identified as being the changing status of identity as a reflexive project and, increasingly, the role of consumption within this process (Bauman, 2000; Giddens, 1991). These processes place the individual at the centre of his/her own life experience and as responsible for determining the trajectory of his/her personal biography. Recognizable and dependable traditional sources of authority are eroded, leaving the individual with the onus and responsibility of making personal life choices in a field of transient, competing and contradictory meanings. 'Individualisation consists in transforming human identity from a *given* into a *task* – and charging the actors with the responsibility for performing that task and for the consequences (also the side effects) of their performance' (Bauman, 2001: 144). Bauman's (2000) postmodern interpretation of liquid modernity concerns the response of individuals to this pluralized and fluid array of choice. He suggests the late-modern conditions of liquidity lead to the inevitable focus upon the objects of production – commodities – as sources of meaning. It should be noted that within post-Fordist systems of production and with the rising significance of the service economy, commodities no longer represent physical objects alone, but also ephemeral signs and spaces (Lash and Urry, 1994).

Due to the significance of experience within this framework (for shaping the self) the focus here is on social interaction. The interactionist perspective stresses the active, creative components of existence, while acknowledging that society and the self are conceptualized as co-present realities (Atkinson and Housley, 2003). The self is foundational, conversational in intent, and the nodal point of a dialectic between an 'I' and a 'me' representing the ongoing construction of the self in a social space. Stated simply, society shapes the self and social behaviour. But in a world that increasingly mediates between the self and society, the proliferation of discourses, processes of globalization, the rise of the amorphous multinational corporations, regional and global multiculturalism, collapsing political and symbolic spaces and the rapid compression of space and time, self-identity becomes increasingly problematic. According to Castells (2004), in a network society, identity becomes much more open and porous because of the connections made possible by global communication. Contemporary identities rely less and less on tradition and more on social interaction; although this interaction does not necessarily require a physical co-presence. It is in this context that interactionist theorization is squarely placed, a heterogeneous social field of multiplicity, flux and mobility that posits a formative and 'solid' self. The explosion of identities, identity politics, core selves, male selves, female selves, transsexual selves, dream selves, transcendent selves, ecological selves and so on, is all part of the self in a 'network economy' (Castells, 2004). Of course, one of the issues here is that not everyone has access to this 'network'.

Tourism can provide the traveller self with profound centres of meanings and symbols endowed with cultural significance which are in some ways different from their own environments (Brown, 1992). As Pearce (1990: 32) observes, 'meeting new people, making friends and expanding one's view of the world through these contacts' is an integral aspect of contemporary tourism. Indeed, the concept of tourism itself is constituted by negotiated identities of the tourist self and the other, where the symbolic logic maps meaning systems into networks of self–other. Social theory, and specifically interactionist theory, thus offers useful insights into the nexus of relations inherent in the cross-cultural exchange between the selves of the tourism experience (Wearing, 2001; Wearing and Wearing, 2001). The traditional primacy of a conceptual division between theory and practice has held sway in tourism; the contemplation of the world as it exists to be known 'out there'. However, deconstructive sociologists such as Game (1991) have shown that theory has been understood as a reflective knowledge, a mirror of the real, a representation that denies its own desire and mediation. Tourism theory was developed within a tradition that relied on a Cartesian rationality, a speculative knowing that is exclusive of the other (for instance, culture) and disregards new ways of knowing. Paradoxically, such knowledges of tourism excluded other cultures and the realm of nature (Hall and Tucker, 2004; Hollinshead, 1998).

An understanding of the self in travel, and its representation, arises through the desire to hold still the flux of meaning in order to master and know it. The organization of leisure and, by association, tourism has overwhelmingly been structured by the desire for knowledge as stable truth and reflection in the asking of questions such as 'What is a tourism experience?' Contemporary theory has moved questions about meaning into a different order of analysis, with particular reference to writing the body, deconstructing binary oppositions and decolonizing truths. Mead (1934) attempted to bridge the gap between the self and those constructed in interaction as 'significant Others', 'significant reference groups' (both positive and negative), and the 'generalized Other' of social and cultural values. In so doing, he allowed for a selective interaction between a knowing agent and dominant forces in an individual's immediate milieu. In his schema, cultural space formed an important part of this process, and the 'Other' could also become an important part of the self if perceived to be significant. By elaborating on Mead's conceptions using Giddens's (1991, 2006) notion of an increasingly socially reflexive self, it is possible to incorporate otherness into the experiential identity that is constructed from the interplay of the self in tourist space.

Stories and Narratives

Recounting stories and narratives of travel (through diaries, stories to friends, photographs, emails and the like) is central to the tourism experience and to the construction of the traveller self. These can be viewed in some way as forms of self-fashioning. In this sense, the processes of travel involve the reconstruction of identity and the 'narrativisation' of the self (Desforges, 2000). On a more mundane level, the narratives that are constructed from the practices of tourism consumption are ways of organizing both experiences and expectations, of working with them to reflexively produce coherent accounts (Giddens, 1991). The ways in which tourist consumption involves, among other elements, some form of reworking of the self – of incorporating new experiences of places and forms of travel into biographical, narrative accounts – have increasingly been examined empirically by tourism researchers (see, for example, Desforges, 1998, 2000; Elsrud, 2001; Li, 2000; Meethan et al., 2006; Noy, 2004).

In many ways, the narrative acts as an organizing principle that shares some analogous formal properties with travel, migration, intercultural exchange and, in particular, the temporal sequence of departure, arrival and return (Robertson et al., 1994). As with the gaze, what we are dealing with are a number of cultural elements that frame representational forms and expectations (Clifford, 1997; Galani-Moutafi, 2000; Hall, 2000; Robertson et al., 1994). Markwell and Basche (1998: 228) similarly note that the narratives of travel and self recounted in personal diaries are 'no doubt … edited version[s] of the reality … experienced, filtered … through an array of social and cultural "lenses", just as the holiday photo album tends to feature the "good times" rather than images of negative or mundane experiences'. Yet, as Skultans (1998) demonstrates, self-narratives do not passively reflect the structure or content of discourses or literary texts; they are 'undoubtedly a vehicle for shared cultural representations', although they also involve 'imaginative truth and creativity' (1998: 27). In order to be intelligible, narratives, like other forms of experience, must be rendered into forms that are both culturally specific and common. This ordering and accounting for experiences is an active rather than a passive process, in which people interpret, negotiate and create their own particular meaning (Skultans, 1998).

Giving voice to experience is an important process discussed by Desforges (2000). Drawing on the work of Giddens (1991), Desforges (2000) argues that the significance of biography in relation to self-identity has both internal and external elements. The former refers to the ways in which an individual constructs a dialogue with themselves, and the latter the ways in which this dialogue is presented to the outside world. Desforges explores narratives of traveller identity to gain an individualized understanding of selfhood. In considering the increasingly subjective nature of formative experiences, attention is directed towards the ways in which travellers actually experience social reality, where this experience is actively produced rather than merely obtained. The role of long-term travel in providing 'authentic' experiences of the other and of the self consists of a series of opportunities for escaping the restrictions of previous identities and providing experiential material for the reconstruction of self-identity. Travel experiences are thus drawn upon to re-imagine and re-define the self.

The transitional nature of youth, from adolescence to adulthood, is commonly associated with the redefinition of self-identity, which for young people is often constituted by experiences of anxiety and the possibility for change, or 'fateful moments' (Giddens, 1991). Desforges (2000: 936) argues that many young people consider travel as a rite of passage that 'provides answers to questions that are raised about self-identity at fateful moments'. Therefore, long-term independent travel is simultaneously considered as educational and character-building, and 'is imagined as providing for the accumulation of experience, which is used to renarrate and represent self-identity' (Desforges, 2000: 942). Similarly, Elsrud (2001: 598) describes the travel experience as a process of narrating self-identity. Drawing on Giddens's (1991) conceptualization of identity as a 'self-reflexive project', Elsrud regards 'the traveller as narrator and the journey as narrative'. She states that independent travelling, such as long-term global backpacking, is often presented as an adventurous lifestyle, and independent travellers are accredited with increased knowledge, a stronger sense of identity and social status (Elsrud, 2001: 597). These themes are further explored in Chapters 6 and 7 of this volume, in relation to the ways in which new communications technologies and the intersection of the global and the local are framing traveller experiences and the narratives of travel.

Although Desforges (2000) and Elsrud (2001) are focused on a particular group of tourists comprised of long-term independent travellers (or backpackers), Li (2000: 876) observes that even within the
confines of package tours, the potential for the re-imagination of the
self through the experience of travel still exists. Similarly, Gable and
Handler (2000), in their analysis of the heritage museum in Willamsburg
in the United States, note that the production of memory among the visitors is not the simple acceptance of one dominant 'reading' (see also
Mellor, 1991; Raz, 1999), but instead is produced through a complex
process of interaction, often involving family, memories of past visits, and
the purchase of souvenirs (Löfgren, 1999).

The combination of particular localities and forms of local knowledge with the mobile and transient narratives of travel, Otherness and
leisure creates forms of tourism in which the narrative component is
not purchased 'off the shelf' as it were, but rather takes the form of an
active construction of a personal narrative. Authenticity here is an existential condition (Wang, 1999, 2000), a personal experience that is
inalienable (even though this may be mediated through organized and
commodified forms of production and consumption). These considerations are most clearly articulated by Elsrud (2001), who offers an
analysis of the gendered dimensions involved in the construction of
travel biographies. She notes that although women backpackers
appear to be reproducing a Western discourse of travel as adventure
and discovery, they are also entering a masculine world of adventure.
In this sense, they both engage with a particular set of cultural norms
and (through their practical remaking of this discourse and the use of
irony as much as emancipation) construct their own self-identities.

McCabe (2005) also reveals the dynamics involved in the construction of the self in terms of how individuals construct 'being a tourist'
through their experiences and subsequent accounts of these experiences. While rooted in more common discursive forms, these accounts
are also highly personalized and therefore not simple reconstructions
of the gaze. What these examples illustrate is that the dominant
metaphors, discourses and gazes, and the narratives of place created and
sold by the tourism industry, are not the end point; rather they are the
first step which remains to be confirmed, disconfirmed or modified by
subsequent experience (Dann, 1996). Encounters and interactions
with places, people, cultures and environments form the basis for the
development of experiential knowledge. This experiential knowledge
provides a means by which tourists can 'work at' creating their own
personal narratives of the traveller self and the travelled place (Crang,
1997; Jack and Phipps, 2005). Central to this process are notions of

authenticity of place, culture and self (Wang, 2000; see also Chapter 2 of this volume).

Basing his ideas on the existential philosopher Martin Heidegger, Donald Polkinghorne (1988) suggests that human beings are interpretative, temporal, social, cultural, spatial and linguistic entities. This view of human existence posits that self-identity is an ongoing process of creating meaning, which is ordered and expressed according to linguistic characteristics. 'Thus being human is more a type of meaning-generating activity than a kind of object' (Polkinghorne, 1988: 126). Guignon adds:

> Understood as a 'happening' that unfolds throughout a life-time, a person's identity can be grasped only in terms of his or her life story as a whole. The temporal unfolding of life, as Ricœur has pointed out, has the structure of a narrative. (1993: 224–5)

Human beings use their social, cultural and linguistic domains to understand themselves, others and the world as meaningful, as well as retrieving stories that provide models for how actions and consequences are linked. 'Narrative is the discourse structure in which human action receives its form and through which it is meaningful' (Polkinghorne, 1988: 135). The idea that self-identity functions as an unfolding narrative or story is consistent with existential notions of self-identity, because both reject ideas of fixedness and permanence. Authentic self-identity, from an existential perspective, is created rather than being something a person is born with; it is a task or vocation one pursues, which is co-constitutionally defined by one's social and cultural context (Guignon, 2002, 2004). This emphasis on the social and cultural context in existential thinking, that is the emphasis on the Other, is central to the process of a storied and authentic self-identity. Sartre (1948: 45) posits a self-identity whose entity can only be recognized in others, so that human beings create a self out of others' perceptions of the individual. Sartre's ideas here echo Mead's conception of the self (described above), where the 'me' is socially constructed through contact with 'significant others', 'significant reference groups' and the 'generalized other'. In both conceptions, the individual is unable to obtain any truth whatsoever about her/himself, except through the mediation of another. The Other is indispensable to the individual's existence, and equally so to any knowledge that one can have of oneself. Sartre adds:

> Under these conditions, the intimate discovery of myself is at the same time the revelation of the other as a freedom which confronts mine, and which cannot think or will without doing so either for or against me. Thus, at once, we find ourselves in a world which is, let us say, that of 'inter-subjectivity'. (1948: 45)

However, Meethan (2001: 95) suggests that there is a danger in elevating the concerns of the individual above the social and material elements from which they are constructed, suggesting that authenticity is 'a constructed value, or set of values, but cannot be accounted for without considering the social and material contexts in which it is located'. Given the various domains of existential authenticity – interpretative, temporal, social, cultural, linguistic, spatial – the concept of tourism authenticity is essentially invalid for objects and constructs, since what each tourist experiences is either a static or dynamic sense of self-identity in their travels. Following Meethan (2001: 90), we suggest that authenticity 'needs to be seen as a category that is created and recreated in contingent circumstances, sometimes serving to uphold political or ideological positions as much as catering for the tourism market'.

Conclusion

In this chapter we have explored the link between self-identity and tourism to provide a framework for understanding their role in developing the cultures of travel. Our initial discussion focused on the work–leisure binary and the construction of commodified time, which places constraints on the range of experiences and the potential for self-enhancing leisure and tourism. Indeed, the commodification and rationalization of leisure and tourism alienates the tourist by creating desolate two-dimensional experiences negating a deeper understanding and interaction with alternative peoples, environments, cultures and societies. Tourism, from the perspective of the work–leisure binary, is packaged into the ultimate image, where the experience itself rarely lives up to the advertised perfection.

In order to open up the sphere of tourism we argue for an understanding of tourist cultures based on social interaction, which provides a way of mapping the changes in self-identity and individual meaning systems based on the process of self–other. We have suggested here that Mead, and the more recent work of others, such as Giddens on self-reflexivity, can underpin such an approach to leisure and tourism.

Tourist cultures, conceptualized as social interaction, challenge the work–leisure binary, the model of tourism as merely an escape from the shackles of labour. In its stead, a conceptualization of tourist experiences as social interaction provides an understanding of the ways in which the self is reworked in the space of tourism; where it encounters and negotiates alternative peoples and environments that influence the ongoing narrative construction of the self. Self-work in tourism involves reworking old and incorporating new stories into the self that contain both internal and external elements; where intercultural exchange creates new ways of thinking, feeling and behaviour. In the next chapter we build on and extend this approach to theorizing tourism through a discussion of the Others of tourism. In particular, we are interested in the relationship between tourists and the people of the toured locations.

4

Encountering the Other

In order to further frame an understanding of tourism and the development of the traveller self through the lens of the travel experience, it is necessary to consider the significance of encounters with the Others of tourism in this process. The starting point for many investigations of these host–guest relationships has been to consider them in terms of travel from the West to developing nations (see, for example, Bruner, 1991; Mies, 1993; Mowforth and Munt, 2003; Smith, 1989; Smith and Brent, 2001). Such work has highlighted the unevenness of this relationship and suggested that not only does the Western tourism industry often operate with little regard for the social, cultural and economic effects of tourism on developing nations, but the resulting host–guest encounters are also frequently exploitative. The majority of tourists are from Western industrialized nations travelling to destinations in both Western and non-Western nations (Mowforth and Munt, 2003). These tourists from the West thus consume the people, places, cultures and resources of the visited place. MacCannell (1992) described this process as cultural 'cannibalism'. More recently, attempts have been made to move beyond narrow explanations of the host–guest dichotomy to examine the complexities of these relationships (see, for example, Doron, 2005; Harrison, 2003; Maoz, 2006; Scheyvens, 2002). In so doing, the focus has moved away from notions of invasion and exploitation towards trying to understand the process as interactive and contingent.

This chapter begins by examining the tourism relationship between the travellers from 'developed' (touring) nations and the people and cultures encountered in 'developing' (toured) nations. The chapter goes on to discuss the interactions between hosts and guests that give shape to a richer understanding of the tourism relationship and the tourist experience. More specifically, gender is introduced as an important but often overlooked dimension framing the travel experience. We suggest that a particularly insightful but slightly irregular aspect of the interaction between hosts and guests is sex tourism and, by extension, the phenomenon of Western women travelling to developing countries for the purpose of having sexual encounters with local men. This discussion highlights the complexity of the relationship between hosts and guests, suggesting that power operates in negotiated and non-linear ways to disrupt common assumptions, including those associated both with gender roles and the traveller self.

(Inter)Cultural Dominance

A common consequence of mass tourism has been the colonization by Western visitors of some of the most beautiful and sacred spaces of developing countries, many of which have been acquired by wealthy foreigners and transnational tourism operators in order to offer cheap package holidays (Brammer et al., 2004; Meethan, 2001; Urry, 2002; van Egmond, 2007). Tourism is often distorted and skewed in favour of the (relatively) rich and powerful, whose interests control the destiny of many local communities as well as exerting a pervasive symbolic influence over toured cultures and ways of life. A method for analysing this cultural domination is through the concept of hegemony, which provides a way of understanding the relationship between wealthy foreigners, local communities and their places in the developing world.

The concept of hegemony was originally discussed by Gramsci (1971) to provide an explanation as to why communist revolutions did not occur in those countries in industrialized Europe where it was most expected. Gramsci claimed that it was the capacity of the elite (political and business leaders of a modern capitalist society) to subordinate the wider population into accepting and internalizing their moral, political, economic and cultural values that assisted in maintaining social order and circumventing the possibility for revolutionary exchange. Arguing that the ruling class was able to exercise influence over the thinking, motivations and aspirations of the working classes, Gramsci postulated that state control is exerted through a mixture of coercion and spontaneous consent. Thus, it was suggested that the failure to overthrow the capitalist ruling classes and redistribute wealth was due to implicit and explicit offers of the possibility of freedom through increased wealth and material consumption.

In the study of tourism, the concept of hegemony has been used to analyse the cultural domination of 'developing' countries by more powerful Western 'developed' nations. In particular, it has also been employed to better understand the influence of these 'developed' nations on the construction of local destination cultures as Other – as subordinate and inferior to the tourists' own cultures – even while offering opportunities for viewing difference and diversity (Aitchison, 2001; Favero, 2007; van der Duim et al., 2005; Wearing and Wearing, 2006). Within tourism studies, hegemony is used to refer to the way that those with power, most often modern tourism corporations, have been able to commodify and discursively construct tourist spaces and cultures with the consent of local populations. The result is objectified destinations representing cultural exoticism for the gaze, fleeting pleasure and individualized escape of visiting tourists (Urry, 2002). Certain cultures and destinations are constructed as 'exotic', as set apart from the modern and where the tourist can encounter a 'primitive' Other in a natural and authentic 'habitat' (Meethan, 2001: 13, 16). Aitchison et al. (2000: 123) observe that 'within tourism, the creation of a unique place or tourist destination frequently employs the social construction of the Other'. They argue that the outcome is making 'visible the ... dichotomy or dualism between the self and [the] Other, [between] production and consumption, and inclusion and exclusion' (Aitchison et al., 2000: 171).

Central to the Western tourism enterprise is the cultural power to construct the tourist space while ensuring that there is enough of the local culture present (in a sanitized form) to excite and titillate. In this way hegemony is maintained while the exotic (Other) culture is packaged and sold as a viable and valuable commodity. For example, Ponting et al's (2005) work, using the Mentawai islands of Indonesia as a case study, illustrates how the surfing fields that surround these tropical islands are constructed and sold as a surfing 'wonderland' or 'nirvana' by a foreign-controlled surfing tourism industry. The construction of this 'wonderland', they argue, has been communicated through a triangular marketing synergy between foreign surf-tour operators, foreign surf media and foreign surf-wear manufacturers. The local population and environment provide an adventurous backdrop for an adrenaline-filled escapade. According to the work of Timothy and Ioannides (2002), it seems that such synergies are quite common within international tourism. Timothy and Ioannides examined the traditional hegemonic dialogue that occurs in North–South tourism. They argued that these interactions have resulted in strong dependency relationships between developing destinations and multinational companies from developed nations. Through this relationship, the authors claim developing destinations internalize the logic of commodification, where they come to trivialize their own culture as a commodity to be packaged and sold.

The exotic indigenous cultures of both 'developing' and 'developed' nations are thus promoted as commodities of difference to fulfil a commercially created need in the consciousness of affluent tourists, or 'authenticity-seeking' tourists, including backpackers and other independent travellers (Smith, 2003; Young, 2005, 2008). Indeed, as Urry (2002: 1) has noted, tourist gazes 'are constructed through difference'. Many commentators are critical of the creation of commodities of difference through the rearrangement and trivialization of cultural ceremonies, festivals, arts and crafts to meet the expectations of the tourist (for example, Cohen, 2001; Edensor, 1998, 2000; Lash and Urry, 1994; Silver, 1993; Urry, 1995, 2002, 2005). However, there is, of course, a counter-argument that such commodification has actually aided the preservation of some cultures (for example, Bruner, 1991; Harrison, 2003; Taylor, 2001). The ways in which culture is sold to, and consumed by, visitors are a topic of much debate. According to Macleod, 'globalized cultural experiences' are being produced by the tourism industry:

> [T]ourists ... will remain less aware of the destination culture than may be desirable due to the inadequate marketing material that focuses on tried and tested successful formulaic images and narratives. ... If the tourist experience is to lead to a richer understanding of other cultures, and an increased chance for indigenous communities to successfully use their culture as an asset if they wish, then those responsible for selling the destination should become increasingly sophisticated and sensitive towards the meaning of culture and the profile of the tourist. (2006: 83)

At a macro-social level, the systematic commodification and economic dependency of host cultures ensures the maintenance of a cultural hegemony by more powerful developed countries (Britton, 1996; Brohman, 1996; Leung, 2002). At the micro-social level, host communities are in a constant struggle to reinterpret their culture as Western values and beliefs, most notably individualism and consumerism, become more pervasive. This has led to changes in language, dress, body movement, gesture and eating habits in many local communities. These processes of cultural change that impact upon the social and cultural fabric of the host society have been described by Smith (2003) as acculturation (permanent cultural change) and cultural drift (temporary behavioural change that takes place at the time that tourist and local cultures are in contact).

Macleod (2004), for example, found through a study of tourism in the Canary Islands that there was a marked division between the generations of locals born before 1980 and those born after, which is when the tourism industry at this destination rapidly expanded. Macleod argues that the younger generation has assimilated the changes that tourism has created because of their greater exposure to Western television, advertising, films and music. The lifestyles of younger people in the Canary Islands now reflect Western styles of dress, music, speech and aspirations. Similarly, evidence of changes in culture at the micro-social level can be found in Mbaiwa's (2004) study of the Okavango Delta, Botswana, where safari tourism has become very popular. Despite this popularity though, Mbaiwa notes that the industry has had a number of questionable socio-cultural effects, including the breaking down of traditional family structure, increases in crime and prostitution, and the adoption of Western safari-style dress and the traditionally unacceptable Western language, which is now commonly spoken by its young people. It is important to note that tourism is only one of a number of global factors that impact upon the lifestyles and traditions of local people. Social change, brought about through contact with the West, occurs not only through tourism, but also through communications and information technology such as television, movies, advertising and the internet. Negative socio-cultural impacts, such as those described above, have been well documented in the tourism literature, particularly with reference to mass tourism.

For instance, in developing nations, the indigenous inhabitants are often used as servants by the tourism industry. MacCannell (1992) refers to this as a cultural 'cannibalism' – one that eats itself up and potentially self-destructs. The tourist culture assumes the form of a powerful hegemony which submerges, ingests and eventually eclipses the Other culture of the host nation. What began as an attraction of difference and otherness becomes merely incorporated as more of the same dominant culture with the importation of new and dominant (and often homogenized) identities and values. Western hegemony has fundamentally altered the cultural landscape of many destination spaces and the more that tourists are attracted to a region the more likely it is that the destination will attract global capital and a tourism infrastructure. The nature of this investment means that, with time, destinations begin to resemble each other to the extent that they cease to differ from home (MacCannell, 2001; Ritzer, 2006). In this scenario, the traveller self who returns home is one that is reinforced by a sense of cultural superiority which has been constructed around the hegemony of the home culture. The tourist culture dilutes the local culture, so that the selves of the locals are reinforced through the interaction with tourists. However, theirs is a reinforcement of identities that represent sub-servience and inferiority. MacCannell (1992) discusses the interaction between 'moderns' (tourists from 'developed' nations) and 'ex-primitives' (locals from 'developing' nations), arguing that the dominant white Western culture empowers tourists in their desire to consume, devalue and subsume the local culture:

> Cannibalism in the political-economic register is the production of social totalities by the literal *incorporation* of otherness. It deals with human difference in the most direct way, not merely by doing away with it, but by taking it in completely, metabolizing it, transforming it into shit, and eliminating it. The metabolized 'other' supplies the energy for auto-eroticism, narcissism, economic conservatism, egoism, and absolute group unity or fascism, now all arranged under a positive sign ... (MacCannell, 1992: 66)

In his analysis of the documentary *Cannibal Tours*, MacCannell (1992: 25) shows how such representations of wealthy 'tourists on a luxury cruise up the ... Sepik River, in the jungles of Papua New Guinea' is both a physical and metaphorical journey into the 'heart of darkness'. The tourists consume yet frequently misunderstand and generally undervalue what the ex-primitive or Other in that region has to offer them (MacCannell, 1992). Thus, the dominant tourist culture, aided by strategically positioned local entrepreneurs, consumes and homogenizes the local culture. As a result, Western culture is reaffirmed in its restrictive dimensions and its constraints, and prejudices are projected to varying degrees on to the subjectivities of locals. MacCannell (1992) points to the use of language to illustrate the sense of otherness and inferiority attributed to those of differing ethnicity. For example, when we 'refer to traits and characteristics that are attributed to others as "ethnic" ... [such as] "I am—; you are—; he is—" ("black," "Chicano," "white," and so on)', thus constructing the third person as Other and most often inferior to 'us' (MacCannell,

Table 4.1 Hegemonic constructions and cannibalistic tourism

Concept	Western society	Local community
Power	Economic resources	Economic dependence
Culture	Hegemonic control (control of local culture by the West)	Hegemonic acquiescence (tourist culture pervades own)
Values	Capital investment and profit	Survival, profit and employment
Place/space	Tourist destination a tourist space, an image	A place on display (home and everyday life)
People	Tourists as voyeurs	Locals as servants and objects for observation
Selves, 'I', 'me'	Constrained by hegemonic culture, consumes and eliminates Others	Constructed as 'they', 'other', 'inferior' to the tourist culture

Source: Wearing and Wearing (2006: 160) 'Rereading the subjugating tourist in neoliberalism: Postcolonial otherness and the tourist experience', *Tourism Analysis*, 11 (2): 145–63. Reproduced with permission.

1992: 125). Yet, MacCannell does not want to do away with difference. Rather, he wishes to retain the specificity of individual cultures while allowing subjectivities which transcend parochialism and cultural determinism with contributions from both moderns and ex-primitives (MacCannell, 1992, 2001). The tourist enterprise thus becomes an arena for contesting cultural hegemonic dominance, a space for genuine interaction between the cultures of hosts and cultures of guests. Table 4.1 shows the six key factors that are said to comprise the hegemonic construction of tourism.

The model of tourism that Wearing and Wearing (2006: 160) develop builds on MacCannell's (1992: 68) ideas of differentiation from the 'savage', 'aggressiveness' of corporations' 'cannibalistic' promotion of 'incorporation' to one that is based on one of *interaction*. In their model, MacCannell's neo-nomads of tourism move across cultural boundaries, not as invaders, but as imaginative travellers – as *chorasters* – who benefit from a displaced self-understanding and the freedom to go beyond the limits that their own cultural frontiers represent. One element that is essential here is the idea of hybridized and unfixed cultural identity formation. Wearing and Wearing (2006), drawing on the work of Goffman as well as postcolonial approaches (such as Bhabha, 1994; see Chapter 7 of this volume), see tourism to and from the Western world as an opportunity to form hybrid cultures. As Aitchison et al. (2000: 171) note, 'people and places are engaged in constantly evolving processes of interaction and "remaking" of the world around them'. Similarly, Desforges (1998) documents this process in his discussion of the emergent 'planetary consciousness' of independent travellers.

The formation of hybrid cultures, then, becomes a precondition for inventive representation in creating subjectivities which resist cultural constraints and cultural determinism. The result is that the tourists and locals in hybridized cultures can have possibilities to cross over their own cultural boundaries – the tourist not as an invader, but as an engaged traveller; and the local not existing in a static culture, but engaged in a dynamic and evolving culture (MacCannell, 1992; Wearing, 1998). This is the sort of interaction that Bauman envisions when he speaks of tourism as a 'springboard' to cross-cultural interaction and coexistence (Franklin, 2003). He observes:

> Politically, ethically, socially it's a very, very important experience – to be attracted to otherness, to be inclined in some sense to get to know something you didn't know before, to go where you were not before, and so on. In our times particularly, crowded together on a full planet, we face the need to rise to that challenge more than ever before. … Curiosity of the 'otherness' could be … an excellent springboard to gather momentum in that long and arduous venture [toward discovering] … a mode of coexisting. (Franklin, 2003: 214–15)

The face-to-face interactions that occur between tourists and locals can then be conceptualized as a space where the tourist or community member is able to challenge the way in which culturally specific discourses construct the 'I' and 'you' of their cultures in opposition to the 'other' inferior ethnic, indigenous or national cultures (MacCannell, 1992; Wearing, 1998).

Hosts and Guests

Host–guest relationships have been the subject of much research and theoretical debate within the study of tourism (Aramberri, 2001; Smith, 2003). The origins of the study of hosts and guests emerged from anthropological concerns with the impacts of tourism on local cultures, and since the 1970s researchers have been concerned with the subsequent conflicts that can arise, and the tensions that exist, between visitors and locals. One of the earliest edited works in the academic literature on the anthropology of tourism was the pioneering work of Smith (1977). Smith's book comprised a collection of essays examining host–guest relationships and cultural impact studies of tourism in a number of (predominantly non-Western) nations. A concern was directed towards the economic benefits that local communities can gain from being involved in tourism as well 'the nature of tourism and its effect on the structure of society' (Smith, 1989: ix).

Due to its origins in anthropological and ethnographic research, the host–guest paradigm focused primarily on interactions between hosts in pre-industrial societies and tourists of developed nations (Aramberri, 2001). As a result:

> Few large industries evoke such close, face-to-face contact between people of different means, class, ethnicity, religious, and cultural backgrounds. Few human activities have such a great potential for exposing on a personal level the considerable inequalities that do exist between people, particularly between people of different countries and different color. (Chambers, 1997: 1)

The direct and personal contact between people of different socio-economic positions and cultural backgrounds that the tourism industry produces is a defining element of our conceptualization of tourism in terms of interaction. The capacity of such interactions to expose relationships of inequality that are grounded in race, culture and class is important in unveiling the often concealed power relationships that privilege individuals from the Western industrialized – touring – nations. It is equally important to recognize that the discursive production of the Other, through both language- and image-based representation, can often conceal these power relationships and frequently elicit tourist desire precisely through the notion of difference. In saying this, it is clear that the capacity of tourist-based interaction to expose relationships of power and inequality is, in fact, predicated on the reproduction of those inequalities. It is in this way that Mowforth and Munt (1998: 49) suggest that tourism can be viewed as a 'conduit for relationships of power', and Morgan and Pritchard claim that: 'Tourism processes *manifest power* as they mirror and reinforce the distribution of power in society, operating as mechanisms whereby inequalities are articulated and validated' (1998: 7).

Developments in research regarding power and tourism have inspired questions in relation to the impacts that tourism as a global industry can have on various societies and cultures. Whereas tourism has long been positioned as an industry which can alleviate the economic problems of nations, regions and cities (Craik, 1991, 2001; Robinson, 1999), an increasing body of research now acknowledges that tourism is a complex phenomenon that can result in a tapestry of social and cultural problems as well as benefits for host societies and cultures (Craik, 1991). The transition in both theoretical and empirical focus towards examining the complex and diverse social and cultural impacts of tourism on travelled cultures is evident in the 'knowledge-based platform' that developed from the 'advocacy platform' of tourism studies (Jafari, 1989; see also Chapter 1 of this volume). Dann's (1996) identification of the 'conflict perspective' explicitly acknowledges the systemic inequalities, and relationships of domination and subordination, that exist between the toured (host) and touring (guest) cultures that are perpetuated by the tourism industry.

Thus, tourism is recognized as a significant phenomenon that reflects and reinforces global power structures and particular relationships within and between societies, especially those relationships that are 'grounded in relations of power, dominance and subordination which characterise the global system' (Morgan and Pritchard, 1998: 3). Power relationships, particularly in relation to colonialism and imperialism, are exemplified through tourism discourses. Some of the dominant ways in which power operates within contemporary tourism include: the dominance of the 'first' world over the 'third' world and the perpetuation of uneven and unequal relationships (see, for example, Mowforth and Munt, 1998); the view that tourism is an extension of earlier imperialistic and colonial ambitions of Western nations (see, for example, Chambers, 1997; D. Nash, 1989; Palmer, 1994); the representation of indigenous people (see, for example, Morgan and Pritchard, 1998; Young, 2009a); and, as discussed below, the phenomenon of sex tourism.

The mythology of the Other is fundamental to much tourism. For instance, Selwyn (1996: 10) argues that 'the tourist imagination' is configured on the basis of 'ideas, images, myths and fantasies about the Other'. Similarly, Fullagar has observed that:

> Desire moves us towards that which is different, unknown and other to the self … as a movement in-between home and away, familiarity and uncertainty, travel is a liminal space inhabited by *multiple* desires that can produce different ways of knowing self and other. (2002: 57)

In relation to a tourist desire to experience Other cultures, Wang notes that:

> Tourism involves interaction and an antithesis between the touring (subject) and the toured (object). The touring, or the tourist,

as an agent of modernized society, comes to be a subject. In contrast the toured, often in the form of the exotic, difference, or novelty, becomes an object of curiosity at which tourists gaze. (2000: 218)

The interactions between hosts and guests give shape to the tourist experience. Various researchers have suggested that particular forms of tourism will have significant effects on the cultures and societies of toured destinations, and particular types of tourist will have varying levels of interactions with local communities. For instance, Smith (1977, 1989) discusses tourism and tourist typologies as a way of understanding the impacts of tourism, observing that:

Dependent upon the type of tourism, the expectations of the tourists, and the host's ability to provide appropriate facilities and destination activities, the effects of tourism can be assessed along a continuum from a highly positive relationship that benefits all, to a highly disruptive, negative interaction fraught with conflict. (1977: 4)

This way of thinking is reminiscent of the perceived utility of typologies that was prevalent at the time. While there is substantial merit in this conceptualization – particularly in understanding that certain types of tourist will have differing degrees of interaction and relationship with local cultures – it also has clear limitations. As we discussed in Chapter 2, differentiating tourists based on type and activity can be counter-productive because such conceptualizations promote a simplified way of looking at travel and the travel experience that can obscure complexity and encourage the pigeon-holing of people and situations. Despite this critique, the host–guest issue remains a central problematic within tourism studies.

Recent contributions to the debate on hosts and guests have questioned the legitimacy of presenting these categories as a binary opposition, and have suggested that the host–guest relationship is complex and its blurred nature needs to be considered and interrogated (Aramberri, 2001; Sherlock, 2001). Sherlock (2001) explores the ways by which distinctions between hosts and guests are contested, and how these distinctions alter over time. In her case study of Port Douglas, a popular tourist town in Queensland, Australia, Sherlock notes the fluidity of the host and guest categories. This destination has a high population of transient and migrant workers. Thus, she found that 'residents' consumption patterns and migration motivations indicate some commonalities between hosts and guests in the town' (Sherlock, 2001: 287). As a result, she argues that individual and collective identities are contested, with guests becoming hosts (as they take on employment in the town) and later becoming guests again (as they move away from the town to tour the local area). The lack of recognition of complexity is one of the greatest challenges to the traditional host–guest paradigm. This is precisely why any discussion of hosts and guests as dichotomous is problematic. Aramberri argues that the host–guest model is a 'myth' and, as such, it 'does not help to explain the nature of modern mass tourism; obscures the complex interactions between local cultures and their environments, and favors a static and exclusionary vision of cultures' (2001: 741).

The ambiguous nature of the host–guest model is further evident in that host–guest interactions have traditionally been discussed from a Western-centric perspective, with critiques based around the relationships between Western tourists and non-Western hosts (Chan, 2006). However, in the past decade there has been significant increases in non-Western tourism, as evident in the growing tourist markets of, for example, China, South Korea and India. As noted by Chan (2006: 187), 'Asian tourism is going to play a leading role in global tourism development as well as in adding to the complexity of global human interactions and cultural transformations'. There is also the vexed issue of the relationship between hosts and guests in the context of domestic tourism that is a rarely considered but extremely important aspect of contemporary tourism.

Tourism requires the commodification of places, people and their material cultures, yet it is precisely this commodification that apparently falsifies social relations, and renders cultures inauthentic – caricatures of themselves. If this formulation is unpacked, it becomes possible to see that it comprises a number of assumptions that need to be challenged. First, it is assumed that cultures are bounded and static entities subject only to outside influences and thus devoid of any internal tensions and dynamics. Second, there is the associated assumption that such outside influences will result in entirely negative encounters between dominant centres (usually, but not exclusively, 'the West') and less powerful peripheries. Third, by counter-posing authenticity and the notion of loss, the authentic is reduced to fragments of the 'real' which are left over from the high point of modernity (Hughes, 1995: 799). Combined, these three scenarios lead to a fourth element – that of romanticizing the 'exotic Other' as somehow being 'true' and 'more real'. In this fashion, traditional ways of life become valorized (Butcher, 1997; Crick, 1989; Roudometof and Robertson, 1998).

If it is accepted that commodification is a consequence of modernity in general, and neoliberalism in particular, then it can be viewed not only as a 'measure' of intrusion, but also as an agent of despoliation which challenges the 'authenticity' of cultures and reduces them to a standardized and undifferentiated mass. The argument is often presented as the inevitable spread of free market and consumerist values through the global expansion of market mechanisms and ideologies. In itself, this common-sense idea that such processes will inevitably lead to some kind of uniform world culture is part of a long-running debate (see, for example, Frow, 1997; May, 1996; Ritzer, 2007). It not only equates the acquisition of affluence with a corresponding loss of authenticity (Miller, 1994), but also invokes notions of a pre-commodified utopia. Within such a conceptualization, supposedly authentic cultural forms that are uncontaminated by the sameness of modernity and the inevitable alienation of capitalism can be discerned (MacCannell, 1976). The problem is often outlined in terms of an irreconcilable paradox or as the inherent ambivalence of modernity itself (Wang, 2000). In relation to the effects of tourism, this is often represented as a fall from grace; no sooner is 'paradise' discovered than it is inevitably overrun by the 'barbarian hordes' (Curtis and Pajaczkowska, 1994; Turner and Ash, 1975).

This notion of invading barbarian hordes takes on a particularly fascinating complexion when considered in the context of gender and travel. When the traveller self is female, dominant notions of the traveller are subverted because in the tourism literature the traveller is routinely coded male. As Rojek and Urry (1997: 16) observed, 'the dominant tradition in travel was and is palpably masculine'. Similarly, Jokinen and Veijola (1997) argue that the literature of travel and tourism is essentially based on the real and fantasized experiences of men. This gendered lens, however, provides a range of important insights into aspects of host–guest relationships, particularly when the host is male and the guest is female.

Gender, Sex and Tourism

Kinnaird et al. (1994: 24) note that tourism 'revolves around social interaction and social articulations of motivations, desires, traditions, and perceptions, all of which are gendered' and gender is a 'key signifier in both the representation and consumption of leisure and tourism landscapes'. Pritchard and Morgan (2000) found that the majority of existing studies of gender and tourism issues focused on sex tourism (discussed below) and economic issues. As a result, 'discussions of gender and gender relations are about power and control' (Kinnaird et al., 1994: 24). Inherent to this debate is the contention that there exists a subversive hegemonic bias towards masculine tourist experiences. As Jokinen and Veijola argue:

> [T]he figure of the tourist is drawn out by merely alluding to abstractions derived from an interplay of male and female morphologies. Hereby the dominant male symbolic order (structuring and structured by the male imaginary) is performed, repeated and supported by the sociological discourse. (1997: 34)

Many feminists would suggest, as Craik (1997: 130) does, that tourism is 'an industry emanating from industrialisation ... transformed by post-industrialisation', being 'particularly male oriented' and emphasizing 'masculine pleasures, priorities and outcomes ... at the expense of other dimensions'.

One need only look at the quintessential tourist escape area, the beach, to realize that:

> If the beach is a place of bodily disclosure, women are called upon to go further than men. In this sense, beach culture might be said to represent male triumphalism for women are incontrovertibly the paramount objects of display. (Rojek, 1993: 189)

The construction of urban and heritage tourism space has also traditionally been gendered and coded as masculine (Aitchison et al., 2000; Markwell et al., 2004). According to Aitchison et al. (2000: 135), 'landscapes of heritage tourism offer gendered and mythologized representations of power that can serve to merge history with heritage and fact with fiction, whether that power be masculinist, nationalist, militarist, or a combination of all three'. Indeed, most models of the urban dweller were based on a mixture of fear and control; and, in particular, the techniques for sustaining control by middle-class urban men when faced with fears of the Other, especially the sexual Other (Jokinen and Veijola, 1997).

In this sense, women are categorized as Other. Certainly, feminist theorists have argued that women have long been constructed as 'non-men' in mainstream social science theoretical debates (Kinnaird et al., 1994). Summarizing the work of Cixous (1983), Aitchison et al. note three fundamental relationships in constructing the Other:

First, the construction of the Other is dependant upon a simultaneous construction of 'the Same', or something from which to be
Other to. Second, this relationship is one of power, whereby that
which is defined as 'Same' is accorded greater power and status than that which is defined as Other. Third, that which is
defined as Other is accorded a gender and this gender is
always female. (2000: 123)

Aitchison (1999, 2001) and Aitchison and Reeves (1998) argue that
tourism, through its association with the exotic and erotic, is a complex medium and mediator of symbolic and material power in the
'othering' of gender. Studies of leisure and tourism experiences of
both males and females indicate that sex-specific activities contribute
to societal definitions of male and female identity, thus in many
ways producing a conformity to gender stereotypes and acting as
a restrictive rather than a liberating influence on identity (Aitchison,
2001, 2005; Samdahl, 1992). Richter (1995) found that the
linking of tourism with sex is rampant in marketing; for instance,
souvenirs often promote women as sex objects, and destination
attractions remain male-dominated preserves. This finding is also
evident in Dickson et al's (2006) study of gendered imagery in the
tourism marketing of Australian ski resorts. They found that the
majority of respondents saw men (as they appeared on snow sports
brochures) as 'active' and 'competent participants', while women
(who appeared on the same brochures) were seen as 'inactive' 'eye
candy'.

   C.M. Hall (1996) argues that mass tourism (in South-East Asia)
has led to the further institutionalization of the exploitation of
women in what are predominantly patriarchal societies:

> [M]odern mass tourism and its accompanying images only
> serve to promote unequal gender relations in which women are
> subordinate to male interests. Tourism will continue to be the
> mainstay of the region's economies. However, while tourism pros-
> titution may decline, the intrinsic inequality of host–guest relation-
> ships in mass tourism can only continue to perpetuate the
> current set of gender relations. (Mass) tourism is sex tourism.
> (C.M. Hall 1996: 277)

Other studies, however, are less pessimistic, suggesting that leisure
and tourism can create a space for a resistance to dominant male discourses and an arena for personal satisfaction and the transcendence of

gender stereotypes (Aitchison, 2001; Cockburn-Wootten et al., 2006; Edward et al., 2001; Poria, 2006; Shaw, 2006; Taylor, 2000; see also Chapters 6 and 7 in this volume). Edward et al's (2001) analysis of female sex tourism in the Caribbean argues that tourism researchers have been too narrow in their definitions of sex tourism as it is applied to women, often emphasizing 'romance' as opposed to 'sex' when labelling and theorizing the phenomenon. Sánchez-Taylor (2000, 2001) argues that the reason for this is that female sex tourism inverts the traditional power relationship in tourism, where males control the exchange process and where sex tourism is expressed as a form of male (guest) power and female (host) powerlessness. Attempts to subsume this inversion include the desexualizing of female sex tourists by viewing them as 'lonely women', or suggesting that female sex tourism is a form of 'romance', making it seem more innocent than it actually is (Momsen, 1994, as cited in Sánchez-Taylor, 2000: 45). Sex tourism, of course, is also a particular expression of the host–guest relationship that is a feature of international travel, particularly involving travel by Westerners to developing countries. It is important also to note that sex tourism is particularly pervasive in developing nations, and 'local and indigenous women and men are often rendered subservient to the needs of wealthy, powerful Western tourists' (Smith, 2003: 50).

While research into sex tourism has traditionally focused on male tourists, Sánchez-Taylor (2000: 46) interviewed female sex tourists travelling in Negril, Jamaica, finding that 'some women travel for sex in much the same way that some men do'. She argues that female sex tourists are 'travelling to cross traditional male domains using traditional male powers to reaffirm their femininity. It is important for many female sex tourists to reaffirm their sense of "womanliness" by being sexually desired by men' (Sánchez-Taylor, 2000: 46). De Albuquerque (1998), following Sánchez-Taylor's line of argument, claims that female sex tourism is viewed by men and the tourism industry as an anomaly. However, female sex tourists have been travelling to the Caribbean since the early 1970s, where they typically purchase a local as an escort for the duration of their stay. While it is impossible to count accurately the numbers of female sex tourists travelling to the Caribbean, there is also an increasing trend of women being involved in tourist-related prostitution in the informal sex sector (Sánchez-Taylor, pers. comm., 4 July 2007).

In a study of female sex tourism, Wearing and Wearing (2006) examined the growing popularity of so-called 'hen weekends', where groups of women, usually from the United Kingdom, travel to

selected cities in continental Europe to 'celebrate' before the immi-
nent marriage of one of the group. As also happens with male 'stag
weekends', the emphasis of this form of tourism is alcohol and sex.
Many hen weekends (whether organized independently or as part of
a package tour) include viewing male strip shows, purchasing male
prostitutes and/or having brief sexual liaisons with local men. Here
again is an example of women using travel and tourism to invert
institutionalized gender (host–guest) roles and to participate in
leisure activities that are typically the preserve of men. Yet this and
other forms of female sex tourism are very often desexualized and
painted as 'innocent fun' (Sánchez-Taylor, 2001), but female sex
tourists 'are not blameless' in the 'dependency relationship' that
exists in the context of sex tourism (Smith, 2003: 50).

Sánchez-Taylor argues that female sex tourism is underpinned by
essentialist constructions of gender and heterosexuality, which blur
the understanding of sexual exploitation and victimhood. She
observes that:

> [I]t is important to recognise that women, as well as men, can
> be sexually hostile and predatory. ... [S]ome women do actually
> take a narrowly instrumental view and impersonal approach to
> sex with local men, and are quite willing to enter into explicitly
> commercial sexual relationships. This group of women is [sic]
> certainly in the minority, but is nevertheless present, and will
> specify its exact requirements as purchasers of sexually objec-
> tified bodies. (Sánchez-Taylor, 2001: 759)

While there are similarities between female and male sex
tourism, there are some important differences, the most obvious
being the far greater vulnerability of female sex workers, when com-
pared to their male counterparts. For example, female prostitutes are
far more likely to be 'cheated, beaten and raped by their [male] tourist
clients', and female prostitutes are far more likely to suffer 'police
harassment and legal prosecution' as a result of their activities
(Sánchez-Taylor, 2001: 761). In contrast, male prostitutes who service
female tourists are much less likely to suffer this type of harassment and
victimization (Sánchez-Taylor, 2001).

Other realms of tourism have also been found to offer women an
arena for resisting the essentialist constructions of gender as they can
use travel and tourism for a personal satisfaction that transcends gender stereotypes (Pesman, 1996). Cockburn-Wootten et al. (2006) found
that independent female travellers were motivated by self-discovery,

enlightenment and/or education, and that travel was seen as an opportunity for a respite from the confines and responsibilities of their normal day-to-day domestic environments. Poria (2006) examined an Israeli lesbian woman's travel experience by analysing her published travel diary. The diary revealed her attitudes towards various spaces (such as her apartment, open spaces near her home, and locations she visited as a tourist). Poria argued that the tourist space – space free from people the author knew – allowed the woman and her partner to live a lesbian lifestyle which enabled the expression of a more authentic self. Jordan and Gibson (2005) found that for solo women travellers, travel experiences are mediated by the 'sexualization of space'.

Conclusion

This chapter has suggested that tourism is not an activity that obfuscates and justifies inequalities of difference between hosts and guests. Tourism is not merely a diversion or amusement, a temporary and unsatisfactory means of escape from the grip of modernity with its desacrilized time, commodification, rationalization and boredom. Rather, the phenomenon of tourism is also a subjective experience of enjoyment, growth and identity formation for many people. The host–guest relationship is pivotal here, and this chapter explored the contradictory place of the Other in the experience of tourism. The chapter began by discussing hegemonic constructions of tourism, focusing on the relationship between developed and developing nations. Such relationships have been found to be inequitable and often destructive, limiting the potential for tourism to act as a sustainable form of development in developing countries. But they can also be surprising and revelatory. It is necessary to understand the ways in which local communities can resist and regain control of their places in the context of tourism, which prompts the question of whether there are alternatives that can enable the relocation of cultural ownership and control to indigenous inhabitants. Significant here is the possibility that interactions between locals and tourists can acknowledge and emphasize valuing as well as providing tourists with unique cultural experiences, thereby shifting the Western constructed Other from the margins of participation and ownership back to the centre. These issues are discussed more fully in Chapter 6 of this volume.

To better understand tourist cultures as experience, the spaces in which tourism and encounters between hosts and guests occur must also be better understood. In Part II of the book, therefore, we are concerned with examining the spaces of tourism. We outline various spatial models in tourism and seek to provide a way of moving towards an explanation that encompasses a diverse range of experiences which occur within the tourist space and which might fall under the banner of tourism. To this end, we seek to develop a more nuanced understanding of space and place, with the aim of opening up the realm of tourism studies for the expression of more freedom for both hosts and guests alike. An understanding of tourism as spatialized makes it possible to see the centrality of interaction and engagement (both co-present and mediated) to the development of the selves of tourism.

PART II

TOURIST SPACES

5

The Landscapes of Tourism

This book has highlighted the significance of the relationship between the travel experience and the identity of the traveller self. Particularly important in this context are relations and interactions with Others that occur within the tourist space. In seeking to go beyond the emphasis within much of tourism studies on the tourist as a *flâneur*, for whom travel is a way of looking at, but not engaging with, predetermined destinations, we have sought to consider travel as a process whereby engaged travellers experience and encounter spaces, places and identities to extend their cultural boundaries beyond those imposed by everyday life. In so doing, we have positioned the tourist or traveller self as an interacting *choraster*. In this chapter we extend this positioning by examining the part played by the places and landscapes of tourism. By moving beyond the self/Other dichotomy (where place is seen as Other), it is possible to develop a fuller and more nuanced understanding of the travel experience in, and through, the travelled space and to appreciate that this interaction has the potential to play an important part in expanding the boundaries of how we understand tourist cultures.

Two significant but very different landscapes are central to the contemporary travel experience and thus to the construction of the traveller self: the natural environment and the city. It is these spaces that are the focus of this chapter. With respect to the natural environment, the chapter canvasses views that move beyond conceptualizing nature as a commodity ripe for exploitation to regarding it as intrinsic to the travel experience and the construction of the traveller self. It is further suggested in this context that there is some evidence to suggest that an engagement with the (natural) places of tourism can afford a greater appreciation of the communities that are visited and subsequently, on returning home, one's own communities/environments.

Consumption of the city as a tourist place similarly reveals a number of contradictory and sometimes challenging sets of engagements. The city is first and foremost a spectacle; it is vast and impersonal, and yet through the experience of tourism it can to some extent at least become knowable and tamed. If nature-based travel is underpinned by the (romantic) possibility of harmony and fulfilment, then travel in the context of the city is frequently discussed in terms of anomie, superficiality and alienation as well as display, stimulation and exhilaration. First, however, it is necessary to discuss the importance of space (and place) to the cultures of tourism.

Tourist Cultures, Tourist Space

Tourism is first and foremost about space. Nevertheless, it has only been relatively recently that tourism scholars have sought actively to understand what the spatial actually means to the tourist experience beyond the idea of destination/location. Tourism is about travel through space to space. It is about movement and transience. The idea of movement has been central to Urry's (2007) sociology of tourism, in which he posits a new 'mobilities paradigm' for understanding the many important social and cultural changes taking place in contemporary society. For Urry, the mobility of people, things, information and ideas has become significant to people's lives and organizations, as well as a prime economic driver of modern liberal democracies, which are built upon systems that permit and facilitate the predictable and relatively risk-free repetition of movement, whether of information or people, through space. As we discussed in Chapter 1, Urry (2002) first investigated movement in relation to tourism by drawing on Michel Foucault's concept of the 'gaze'. Urry's study emphasized the visual nature of the tourist experience (as well as other leisure experiences, such as shopping). He argued that tourists seek out distinctive spaces and objects, which they consume visually, and it is through the act of viewing/gazing that these spaces are transformed into 'sites of consumption'. In the process of transformation from empty space to a 'site of consumption', tourist spaces come to embody commodified discourses articulated through limited forms of social interaction (particularly with locals), personal identity and lifestyle. As we have noted above, however, this conception of the tourist is as an observer *in* space (the *flâneur*). We seek to build on this conceptualization to develop an understanding of tourist cultures and the traveller self as also being constituted through engaged relationships in, and with, the visited space (and its people).

Central to an understanding of the spaces of the traveller self is the issue of power. Indeed, Elden (2001: 120), in his study of Foucault, noted that: 'Space is fundamental in any exercise of power. It is well known that power is central to Foucault's work, and that it is a fundamental focus of his historical studies'. Foucault formulated his concepts of power/knowledge through an analysis of the construction of madness as a disease, and the development of the Western system of prisons. He went on to apply these ideas to other institutional contexts, such as schools, monasteries, hospitals and factories, all of which were designed, organized and produced through changes in spatial relations enacting a new and dominant micro-physics of power/knowledge. In his work on madness, Foucault (1961) illustrated how those citizens of eighteenth- and nineteenth-century France who were deemed deviant, unemployed, insane, sick or politically radical were segregated into asylums, hospitals and prisons where they were excluded from participating in society. Social segregation and exclusion were also effected by the partitioning of outlying districts and streets in larger cities, restricting movement, implementing curfews and carrying out house inspections and locking houses.

Foucault's (1961, 1975) illustration of the historical process of 'othering' documented how 'out-groups' were pushed to the periphery of society, both physically and metaphorically. Space was used as a 'disciplinary' mechanism for policing and controlling elements of the population, which was articulated through 'hierarchical observations', the 'normalising gaze' and the 'examination' (Foucault, 1975). Foucault drew on Jeremy Bentham's now famous notion of the 'panopticon' to illustrate the spatial mechanisms of discipline, and levels of internal and external surveillance. Foucault notes: 'The Panopticon is a machine for dissociating the see/being seen dyad: in the peripheric ring, one is totally seen, without ever seeing; in the central tower, one sees everything without ever being seen' (1975: 201–2). These ideas have been applied to tourism studies by many, including Cheong and Miller (2000), Wearing and McDonald (2002), and more recently by Wearing and Chatterton (2007). Such studies illustrate that the process of commodification (essentially a process of economic rationalization) inherent in the development of tourism leads to the segregation and exclusion of local communities from participating in or sharing the process, functions and economic benefits of the industry. Tourism here is shown to be a 'punitive', 'disciplinary' exercise where space is controlled through the articulation and combination of forces. These include the demarcation of tourist space and the creation of a periphery (typically used to house workers and to act as a trans-portation hub to bring tourists and goods into the tourist site), through financial investment tied to specific commodified outcomes, the application of Western models of professional management, power/knowledge and language, and the employment of Western tourism operators (see also Ponting et al., 2005). In these situations local communities are theoretically, physically and economically excluded by the industry.

Crouch's (1999, 2000, 2001; and with Desforges, 2003) writings on the tourism experience over the past years have focused on leisure and tourism encounters with space and place. For Crouch, space is a multidimensional concept that forms an integral part of the study of tourism and the tourist experience (Crouch et al., 2001). Space, as a fundamental component of social action and social life, can be broadly defined with respect to tourism in two ways. First, space can be material, the context within which tourism occurs and thus includes the artefacts, buildings and physical objects that surround the travelling body. Second, space can be referred to as metaphoric, an imaginative arena which is created and represented in the mind through travel images, experiences and expectations (Crouch et al., 2001). Crouch et al. state that when a tourist interacts with these spa-tial elements a 'kaleidoscope' occurs whereby the two forms of space collide and merge in ways that are inseparable. This integration process is one practice that contributes to the individual nature of tourist experiences. Knowledges are formed and a sense of the world is made through the interactions that take place within the space.

According to Crouch et al. (2001: 254), space 'is a medium through which the tourist negotiates her or his world, tourism signs and con-texts, and may construct her or his own distinctive meanings'. Lew claims that:

> [H]umans structure their experience of the world through the creation of places. We create places through both perception and through hard work. We shape places to reflect our identi-ties, just as much as places influence our opportunities and well being. In much the same way tourism is created and occurs in places. (2003: 121)

The complex and subjective processes by which tourists use their indi-vidual personalities to 'practise' (Crouch, 1999, 2000; Crouch et al.,

2001) and 'perform' (Edensor, 1998, 2000, 2001) tourism have been referred to as the embodiment of space. Embodiment is 'the ways in which the individual grasps the world around her/him and makes sense of it in ways that engage both mind and body' (Crouch, 2000: 63). The process of embodying space is the result of complex social and human encounters, individual negotiations with place and subjective interpretations of such experiences (Crouch, 1999). Wearing and Wearing (2001) contribute to this debate by pointing out that tourists have contrasting personalities and differing identities, and each brings different values, beliefs, expectations and knowledge to the travel process which influence the behaviours, outcomes and experiences of their individual travels. At the same time, however, these values, beliefs and knowledges are shaped by significant cultural and social factors. Craik (1997: 118, original emphasis) points out that all tourism experiences occur 'in terms of prior knowledge, expectations, fantasies and mythologies *generated in the tourist's origin culture* rather than *by the cultural offerings of the destination*'.

In his discussion of the embodiment of space, Crouch (2000: 68) suggests three ways in which 'the subject engages space and space becomes embodied'. First, the tourist 'grasps the world multi-sensually' and encounters the space through their five senses working together – sight, touch, smell, hearing and taste (Crouch, 2000: 68). Second, 'the body is surrounded by space and encounters it multi-dimensionally', with individual perceptions of space being influenced by past experiences, culture, beliefs, preferences and identities (Crouch, 2000: 68). Third, the tourist interacts with the space and imbues his/her personality and behaviour on to the space, thus the space is fully encountered by the body and the tourist 'expresses him/herself through the surrounding space and thereby changes its meaning' (Crouch, 2000: 68).

Through the embodiment of space, it is possible, as has been argued by others, that tourists will gain new insights into their own identities plus develop a greater sense of self. Wearing and Wearing (2001) discuss the social and cultural practices within space with reference to relationships, identities and emotions. They state that 'the actual experience that the tourist has is authentic for her/him and will impact upon the self in a number of ways including both an expansion and a reaffirmation of encultured selves' (Wearing and Wearing, 2001: 153). The conceptualization of the self that is gained through travel is acquired through comparisons and contrasts made by the tourist, between the individual, Others, hosts and the encounters he/she experiences (Crouch,

1999, 2000). Crouch (1999: 2) argues that due to the interactive nature of tourist behaviour, it is more appropriate for tourism to be referred to as a practice rather than a product, and best defined as a way of 'practising space'.

Place is thus a fundamental nodal point in the formation and construction of tourist cultures; crucially, one which is inherently structured around the notion of value for a place both as a physical location and as a place in which encounters occur. The tourist space is a site in which constellations of values and meanings are negotiated, constructed and mediated and where the travel experience is interpreted, developed, rejected and/or refined. As tourism destinations are increasingly subsumed under a rationalizing ethic, their only point of distinction becomes the following of fashions, gimmicks and fads (Hall, 1994; Ryan and Hall, 2001; Seabrook, 2001). The effect of the concentration of a world of commodified images and experiences in a short period of time and space (the holiday) is to overpower, disorientate and hypnotize the individual, while the wealth and colourfulness of the display are appropriate to the need for stimulation of over-excited and exhausted nerves. Travel through time to far-distant exotic destination spaces is held out as 'paradise gained' although the return is never presented as 'paradise lost'; and as incomes in the West have increased, so too has the desire to travel to exotic locations. Central to many such experiences of exotic places are deliberate and incidental encounters with nature/the environment and, indeed, 'eco' or 'nature-based' tourism is one of the fastest-growing segments of the travel industry and thus deeply implicated in the construction of the contemporary traveller self.

Touring Nature

Iso-Ahola (1980) advocates that if we regard the environment as part of the self, then it is more likely to be experienced in that way. Therefore, by separating humans from the environment we are separating humans from themselves. This observation could go some way towards explaining the attraction of natural areas to human societies. It is thought by some that natural areas represent, and are living embodiments of, the past, contributing to a sense of continuity and identity. For many indigenous peoples, this sense of identity is maintained through totemism, which accomplishes not only the kinship and cooperation of humans with nature but also the continuity between past and present (Lévi-Strauss, 1964). Humans are constantly interacting with their environment, adapting it to suit intrinsically human ends (Proshansky, 1973). Responses to natural environments are often obtained through feedback from 'others', and nature's greatest distinction from urban or constructed environments is that it cannot quickly be changed to suit shifting needs or requirements. In these cases, it is argued, the human agent must focus on adapting the self rather than the environment. Thus, the interaction between the individual and the surrounding environment is founded on a relationship of self-control. That is to say the behaviour modification resulting from the apperception of an unmalleable and often hostile environment is one that fundamentally questions the ontological and existential status of the agent him/herself; in short, the very make-up of the value system of the individual is brought into relief.

Ittleson et al. (1974) maintain that the individual is not a passive product of his/her environment, but interacts with it and is in turn influenced by it. As we discussed in Chapter 3, interactionist theories suggest that the individual is an active, thinking entity who is able to construct a meaningful existence and a sense of self from the day-to-day context in which he/she lives: 'The individual experiences himself as such, not directly, but only indirectly, from the particular standpoints of other individual members of the same social group or from the generalized standpoint of the social group as a whole' (Mead, 1934: 138). Pigram (1992), in reviewing research in this area, found that Stankey and McCool's (1985) work suggests that natural settings are of major importance to recreation users; even big-game hunters emphasized the experience of nature, with two-thirds of those interviewed for their study stating that enjoying nature was an important part of their trips (Allen, 1991). Kaplan and Kaplan (1989) report that experiencing the spaces of nature is of central importance to visitors to natural areas. Studies on recreation motivation by Shafer and Mietz (1969) and Fly (1986) also suggest that 'enjoying the natural surroundings' and 'experiencing nature' are the strongest reasons for visiting these environments. Similarly, research into white-water rafting conducted by Hall and McArthur (1991) reveals that although adventure and excitement are significant motivational factors, the most important motivation cited was the opportunity to experience the natural environment.

Theoretical debates on the environment have been structured into three 'currents' that are distinct from one another with respect to the seminal question: that of exploring the relationship between the self and nature. The first current is based on the idea that, by protecting nature, the self is first and foremost protecting itself. The environment is endowed with no intrinsic value here. Rather, this scenario stems from an awareness that by destroying the environment that surrounds us, humanity may be endangering its own existence. Thus nature is taken only indirectly into consideration and is based on a position that may be classified as 'anthropocentric'. This philosophy has also been classified as 'shallow' or 'environmentalist' ecology (R. Nash, 1989). The second current takes a step in the direction of attributing moral significance to certain non-human beings and is the basis of the animal liberation movement. The central tenant of this perspective is that all sentient beings are capable of feeling pleasure and pain and must be considered legal subjects and treated as such (Singer, 1975). The anthropocentric point of view is thus discredited within this framework, since animals are included, by the same token as human beings, within the sphere of moral consideration (R. Nash, 1989).

The third current is to say that nature in, and of, itself has rights. This philosophy is termed 'deep ecology', which is 'ecocentric' (R. Nash, 1989; Wearing and Neil, 1999). These egalitarian philosophies believe 'in a holistic view of nature in which the human being, through the self, is intrinsically connected to all life' (Wearing and Neil, 1999: 14). Thus, a perspective on the environment, and of nature, based in ecocentrism is 'recognition of nature's right to exist in its own right, apart from the benefits humankind can derive from it' (Wearing and Neil, 1999: 13). In tourism studies, ecocentrism is expressed to some degree in ecotourism. The term 'ecotourism' has its origins in the 1980s and 1990s (Russell, 2007) when the development of, and interest in, alternative forms of tourism became prevalent, in response to the 'social, cultural, economic and environmental havoc' (Poon, 1993) associated with mass tourism (see Chapter 2 of this volume). Ecotourism is defined as 'responsible travel to natural areas that conserves the environment and improves the well-being of local people' (the Ecotourism Society, cited in Russell, 2007: 226). Wearing and Neil (1999) argue that ecotourism, combined with the evolution of interactionism, makes it possible to explore the inclusion of nature into the self through travel and tourism; a previously inexplicable phenomenon because of the limited application of theory.

It is possible to identify the ecocentric approaches where the ecological well-being of the whole planet is emphasized regardless of the direct benefits of the human population inhabiting it (Godfrey-Smith, 1980; Leopold, 1949; R. Nash, 1989; Pepper, 1984; Rolston, 1992). Employing ecocentrism to prolong the integrity of natural ecosystems would be in sharp conflict with the predominantly instrumental uses of nature and the overpowering Western utilitarian ideology. Ecocentrism is not an approach that can be applied with officiousness, nor is it politically palpable – it is a philosophy that requires a deep thought process and a change in attitudes towards nature. If the ideas of ecocentrism are applied to travel, it is possible to start to formulate the merging of the treatment of nature as Other with the idea of the traveller self. In the analysis of ecotourism, it is necessary to merge the poles of ecocentrism and anthropocentrism at a junction in order to bring about an acceptance that the self/Other dichotomy is invalid for this form of travel.

Arne Naess and George Sessions (cited in Devall, 1988) extend and frame Leopold's (1949) theme of holism into a manifesto called 'the principles of deep ecology'. They believe that human and non-human life on earth has (intrinsic, inherent) value in itself. These values are independent of the usefulness of the non-human world for human purposes. Drawing on these assumptions, it is now often argued that through travel it becomes possible to develop the self and incorporate these beliefs into a oneness with nature. This view has been expressed by Ceballos-Lascurain in his original definition of ecotourism:

> [T]his person will eventually acquire a consciousness and knowledge of the natural environment together with its cultural aspects that will convert him [sic] into somebody keenly involved in conservation issues. (1992: 1)

Following this view, travel is seen as being able to develop the self/Other ideal to one which opposes the paradigms that dominate Judeo-Christian Western society because it places the spirit and its law above nature (Nash, 1967). The scientific approach of the Enlightenment that triumphed in Europe from the beginning of the seventeenth century reduces the universe to a warehouse of objects to serve 'man' and gives priority to the economy over all other considerations (Holland, 1996). Some commentators, such as Rolston (1992) and R. Nash (1989), wish to inscribe the recognition of the rights of nature within the logic of democratic societies. Ecotourism is possibly an avenue for achieving this – of enabling the Western traveller to move nature away from being a commodified product to becoming an intrinsic part of the self through the travel experience.

If tourists are conceptualized within the traditional theoretical frames that focus on tourism and tourist spaces as commodities, it is not possible to conceive pleasure except as being in some way connected with buying, travelling and spending. The purchasing of a travel package is never directly associated with the destruction of nature or culture through Western tourist contact, the extraction of oil for jet travel, or the misuse of land for tourist accommodation. The invisible patina of the trip was its value, not its contribution to self-development, nature or an indigenous community, although these outcomes may result as by-products. As Bookchin (1982: 23) observes, 'the exploitation of nature is closely linked to human exploitation'. It is now possible to understand Leopold's brevity of thought when he said 'we shall never achieve harmony with land any more than we shall achieve justice or liberty for people' (Leopold, 1949: 263). He noted further that it 'has required nineteen centuries to define decent man-to-man conduct and the process is only half done; it may take as long to evolve a code of decency for man-to-land conduct' (Leopold, 1949: 281).

As attention shifts from the environment to the physiological, it gravitates to other aspects of the self. Slosky (cited in Scherl, 1988) explains that natural areas may create a heightened awareness of the self because there is no escape from experiencing the present – the now. The enhancement of these emotional and physical sensations is said to increase awareness of one's inner capabilities, which in turn increases self-confidence. It is thought that some people who repeatedly seek traveller identities, such as adventurousness, can find that an engagement with natural areas reinforces these identities. The effects of a natural-area experience, however, can go beyond simply the drive for stimulation. Natural areas experienced through ecotourism can facilitate a (re)connection with the traveller self through a process of self-control, resulting in an increase in self-confidence, an increased awareness of one's emotional and physiological sensations and an enhanced perception of freedom. Now that tourism studies is seeking to understand more fully the contours of a human affinity with nature in the context of travel, it is possible to speculate on the diverse reasons why humans look for ecotourism experiences. Tarrant et al. (1994) and Driver et al. (1991) argue that there are benefits to be derived from outdoor recreational experiences and it is only by understanding the physiological and psychological changes that can occur within an individual when they experience nature that these benefits can be seen.

According to Brennan (1996), the elimination of ethics, human freedom, religion and spirituality from the Western worldview – the very elements of experience which empower human beings – has been one of the great contributions to deeply ingraining a feeling of powerlessness into the way travellers think about themselves and nature. He suggests that the sense of nothingness which consumes the psyche in turn means humans consume the earth beyond matters of survival. While this is an extreme view, it does point to the importance of trying to understand observed patterns of traveller behaviour and interactions in natural space. An interactionist perspective makes it possible to recognize the status and significance of others in a social group as a dominant construct, as opposed to research based in psychology and social psychology, which regards the influence of others as peripheral in relation to individual decision-making. Macro-social explanatory frames are rendered variable in micro-social contexts (Clarke et al., 1975).

Where a travel engagement with the spaces of nature and the environment is frequently discussed in terms of romantic and idealized notions such as harmony and the enhancement of self, engagement with the spaces of the city is more likely to be framed in terms of alienation and anomie. Nevertheless, the city is a pivotal site of contemporary tourism and the traveller experience, and thus fundamental to any analysis of the spaces of the traveller self.

Cityscapes of Travel

Cities are among the most visited places on earth. They are both attractions in their own right as well as major entry, exit and transit points for people travelling to a host of other destinations. They are thus sites for the performance of departure, arrival and mobility. Major roads and transport hubs, such as railway stations, play significant roles in this respect. But in an era of mass international travel, airports perhaps occupy the most fascinating and contradictory place in the process of positioning the city within the tourist experience. Indeed, it is increasingly commonplace for a traveller's only experience of a particular city to be of its international airport. Airports are simultaneously both place and non-place. They are located in specific geographical locations, and frequently come to stand for those locales (including for the nation), yet they are curiously detached from their situation in space and time. People moving through the space(s) of the airport are both in, and separate from, their geographical location. Those in transit rarely pass through immigration and thus do not officially enter the city/nation – they remain, instead, in a curious non-place known as 'international territory'.

At the same time as being non-places, airports are charged with the role of speaking to and representing the city and nation to visitors (even those in transit). Central to this process of locating an airport in (its) place is the use of architecture, design and signage. Also important is the range of facilities on offer at the airport. Indeed, from the moment the traveller departs the aircraft and enters the airport space both those arriving at their destination and those in transit will frequently encounter a series of advertisements touting the attractions of the city they have just 'entered'. And even before passengers leave the aeroplane, they will have been welcomed by the pilot and flight attendants to the destination city, and provided with key orienting locational information, such as the current time and temperature at the arrival city. Although serving to welcome visitors to a place, airports also draw on a range of international codes that are universal features of the global travel experience and which have the effect of uncoupling the airport from its situation in place and time. For example, most major airports around the world offer a suite of generic shopping and leisure experiences, including retail and fastfood franchises (such as Starbucks and McDonald's). In this respect, airports are very much like theme parks or shopping malls; they are predictable and legible. As with theme parks and malls, airports can also be disorienting and placeless as a result. However, these universal spaces are frequently co-located with some very place-specific souvenir shops and local landmark retailers; for instance, well-known UK/London stores Boots and Harrods both have outlets at London's major international airports alongside a number of other 'high street' retailers.

In Chapter 1 we discussed conceptualizations of the tourist in terms of the strolling detached *flâneur*. The *flâneur*, of course, was first and foremost an urban phenomenon. He was a denizen of the emerging modern city – a connoisseur of its spaces, which he 'claimed' through the acts of walking and looking. The urban spaces he traversed were those of the city centre; in particular, the spectacular and novel shopping arcades of nineteenth-century Paris, which were precursors to the contemporary shopping mall (Stevenson, 2003). Perhaps, in this respect, the *flâneur* can be regarded not simply as the forerunner to the modern tourist but also as the first truly urban tourist. The *flâneur* consumed urban space at the same time as he created it through movement and the act of looking. On the surface at least, the notion of the *flâneur* as the detached observer seems fittingly to describe the experience of visiting the contemporary city. Cities are impersonal and deeply contradictory places. Guest encounters with hosts are often fleeting and the urban experience can lack meaningful engagements with local people and their places. Cities are also spectacles of architecture, design, image and consumption. Indeed, Donald and Gammack (2007: 45) suggest that it could be that 'the idea of the visual city is central to cultural debates on the nature of modern life'. That said, the importance of the city to contemporary tourism, and the seemingly contradictory nature of the urban tourism experience, make it all the more necessary to understand it in terms of the conceptual-ization of place and the traveller self that goes beyond a merely visual and superficial engagement.

For many cities, tourism makes if not a relatively unimportant contribution to the local economy, then surely an almost incidental one. For others, however, particularly many former industrial (second/ regional) cities, tourism has come to be regarded as central to economic recovery and reclaimed prosperity. Thus politicians and business interests in cities around the world are actively engaged in trying to raise the profile of their city in what has become a crowded global tourism marketplace. To this end, a range of strategies is adopted specifically to mark a particular city as unique and attractive to visitors. The term 'urban tourism' was coined to describe not just the phenomenon of visiting a city, but also a specific range of tourism development strategies and initiatives that invariably involve the reconfiguration or redevelopment of urban space in order to attract visitors. These urban tourism approaches will often be focused on the provision of purpose-built recreational, cultural, leisure and lifestyle facilities and resources which are usually located in a desig-nated tourist precinct or precincts. Increasingly, such precincts, and the facilities on offer within them, are themed in some way – the much cited example here is of waterfront festival marketplace devel-opments which invariably adopt maritime themes to underscore both the location of the precinct and an industrial heritage which may no longer exist (Stevenson, 1998). While sharing many spatial and rep-resentational features, such redevelopments also adopt similar styles of architecture and, as in the example of the airport, are the locations of a predictable suite of facilities and retail outlets. The result can often be that the local and the idiosyncratic are replaced by place-lessness, seriality and anonymity – everywhere becomes anywhere. There is usually little that distinguishes one waterfront redevelop-ment from another. They are sites to be experienced on the surface by the tourist as *flâneur* – places MacCannell would describe as front-stage regions (see Chapter 2 of this volume) and Ritzer and Liska (1997) as evidence of their McDonaldization thesis. In contemporary urban tourism, the superficial and contrived increasingly come to stand for the place.

According to Law (1992) the term 'urban tourism' was originally coined to refer specifically to the contrived repackaging of declining industrial cities into centres for tourist consumption. As Law goes on to point out, however, the resources and attractions on offer in these so-called urban tourism destinations do not necessarily differ all that much from those offered by more traditional tourist centres. Featuring strongly in both types of tourist space will be leisure and recreation sites, such as museums, exhibitions centres and retail outlets. There may also be sporting complexes, restaurants and cinema complexes. Also central to many urban tourism strategies, particularly those that set out to repackage deindustrializing cities and their former industrial spaces for tourist consumption, are special events and festivals. These events can be high-profile and global in their scope, such as the Olympic Games or the Football World Cup, but more usually they are much smaller local events, such as music or community festivals.

Along with the formulation of a range of image-focused place-marketing exercises intended to 'brand' the city as a specific destination, another common feature of the spectacle of urban tourism is the use of design and architecture. Of significance here is the building of leisure and high-cost residential spaces, often located on rejuvenated waterfront sites. For the visitor, engagement with these sites and urban experiences will frequently be highly controlled and mediated. They become engagements with (and in) image and superficiality rather than with the lived reality of urban existence. City 'branding' (Donald and Gammack, 2007) and 'visioning' (J. Robinson, 2006) are two highly significant additions to the contemporary urban tourism/city imaging lexicon.

Tourists also go to cities to encounter high-profile landscapes that are often outside contrived designated tourist zones but are important symbols or markers of the city (Stevenson, 2003). Of note here are the major cities of the world, such as New York, London, Paris and Berlin, which are places that many people visit in part to view and experience their distinctive architecture and landscapes. Images of such landmark cities are instantly recognizable to people around the world even though most people will never have actually been there. This familiarity is the result of being featured frequently in popular culture texts, in particular television programmes and films. The relationship between people and the city is far from straightforward. Stevenson (2003: 3) outlines what she describes as the contradictory relationship that exists between people and urban space, arguing that cities can be simultaneously places of 'exhilaration, fear and apprehension'. Zukin (1997: vii) similarly suggests that cities are 'great as well as fearsome'. They provoke terror and joy. They are places of the known and the unknown, the visited and the deserted. Front stages and vast tracts of suburbia where tourists never venture. And of course the tourist's ability to know any city is limited not simply by their imagination, but also by quite tangible factors, such as time and access. It is in the stirring of these responses that the urban tourism experience moves from being that of the detached *flâneur* to that of the engaged traveller.

In seeking to understand the role that encounters with urban space might play in constructing the traveller self, it is useful to consider Simmel's (1964) insights into life in the modern metropolis. Writing at the beginning of the twentieth century, Simmel saw the 'metropolis' and the anonymity it afforded residents and visitors as liberating in that it fostered freedom of expression, behaviour and thought. For Simmel, the city was 'simultaneously the site of freedom and of isolation' (Stevenson, 2003: 24). In other words, the very factors which separate people from each other are the same ones that make freedom possible. While acknowledging the benefits of living in an urban environment, Simmel also saw risks from constant stimulation and change, which he felt bred a level of indifference and a blasé attitude to life. Gergen (1991) similarly argues that in urban environments human beings are saturated with communication technologies, advertising, mobility, knowledge, people and experiences. These multifaceted assaults can subvert notions of the 'true and knowable' and the individual's 'unified moral core' to such an extent that any sense of self and identity becomes fractured, split into a multitude of competing concepts. Social saturation creates anxiety which individuals cope with by becoming blasé, experiencing all things as equal, rather than as valued and treasured, or avoided and discarded (Ritzer, 2006). But there remains a thirst for difference, to escape to greater excitement which has not been satisfied by the fleeting intense stimulations of the city. Amin and Thrift also draw attention to the relationship between the city and passion/ emotions, suggesting that: '[C]ities have to be seen less as a series of locations on which categorical attributes are piled, and more as forces and intensities which move around and from which, because of their constant ingestions, mergers and symbioses, the new constantly proceeds' (2002: 91).

The desire to engage with the new, the different and the changing, whether deliberately or unexpectedly, makes cities attractive places to visit. This is also what makes the traveller seek the predictable and the packaged – to consume those places that are firmly on the tourist map and are labelled and defined as significant and visitable. The city is rendered legible by the tourism industry. The popularity of (official and unofficial) tourist precincts can be explained in these terms. They are entry points into cities which, without markers, can be disorienting and unknowable.

The emphasis of urban tourism is very much on the city centre, its precincts and attractions, but more recently Halgreen (2004: 143) has pointed to another less obvious aspect of tourism within urban environments – deliberate travels to, and through, 'non-tourist' spaces. This form of urban tourism vividly reveals the traveller self as the outcome of the inherent tensions that exist between the performances of the *flâneur* and those of *choraster* – between seeing and experiencing. The focus of Halgreen's study was tourist visits to the high-rise residential estates which, inspired by the 'radiant city' vision of the high-profile architect Le Corbusier, were constructed in post-Second World War Europe. These estates were regarded at the time as emblems of modernity and symbols of political and 'social optimism' (Stevenson, 2003: 83) and this political and architectural history continues to intrigue. Since the 1970s, however, the high-rise housing estates have come to be regarded as social and urban design failures. They are frequently associated with social disadvantage and dislocation, including unemployment, gang violence and substance abuse. For some, the markers of social breakdown are evidence of the failed dream. They are also the factors which make the estates places some people want to see/experience. Visitors to the estates, however, must deal with the reality that they are not welcome and, indeed, the very act of looking and being there may place them in physical danger. They may also witness violence or other illegal or potentially threatening activities. According to Halgreen:

> Tourism in the suburbs makes clear the complexity of the relationship between the extraordinary and the ordinary, between the attractive and its opposite, the unattractive or the trivial. ... The challenge lies not in exploring a place that no tourist has ever been to before, but in visiting a place that a lot of people would not want to visit. (2004: 153)

Needless to say, the 'act' or 'performance' of being a tourist in such non-tourist (backstage) places is very different from those of being a tourist in traditional or designated urban tourism spaces. Not only can it be difficult to travel to such places, but, once there, tourists are also often uncertain about how to interact with either the space or with the locals. As Halgreen (2004: 145) explains, in spite of deliberately choosing to visit these non-tourist destinations, tourists 'rarely know exactly how to approach them as tourist sights'. These tourists do not seek to engage (except in the guise of a local) because in engaging there is danger. Instead, they seek to look but the act of looking is also potentially dangerous. The traditional urban tourist will engage but often only within designated tourist precincts where they also become part of the urban tourism spectacle as they watch and are watched. Visitors to non-tourist urban spaces, however, seek to do so in disguise, remaining invisible – to watch unnoticed or to be mistaken as locals. They do not want to become part of the urban tourism spectacle.

Conclusion

This chapter considered the complex and uneven relationship that exists between tourists and the spaces and places of the travel experience. We have argued that tourist space is not only a physical destination or location but also a central element in the construction of the traveller self. Tourist space is both claimed and created through the acts of moving and viewing, but it is also engaged with in ways that serve to shape the tourist experience as meaningful. In other words, space within tourism is multidimensional; it is formed at the intersection of context and imagination, and travellers make sense of their experiences at this intersection through their interactions with, and in, the travelled space. When considered through the lens of tourist encounters with nature, many have argued that the traveller experience can be one where local environments and peoples are respected, and enriching human-to-human and human-to-environment interactions privileged. It is less easy to be so idealistic about travel through, and to, urban space. The landscapes of urban tourism are often detached from the lived and the everyday and thus provide the traveller with safe, mediated experiences of the city and its cultures. These precincts and the travel experiences they frame are frequently global and universal in form and content – devoid of meaningful encounters with the local. Increasingly, the interplay between the global and the local has become the most significant factor shaping contemporary tourist cultures and the traveller self. These themes are explored further in the next chapter, which is concerned with understanding the impact of global tourism on the spaces of the local.

6

Global Tourism, Local Cultures

Contemporary tourist cultures and associated traveller identities develop and are experienced in the context of complex global networks and interactions. As more and more cities and nations around the world actively seek to be part of this global tourism phenomenon, there is a need to examine the ways in which potentially homogenizing trends and processes affect host cultures and shape the traveller experience and, by extension, the traveller's sense of self. In particular, it is necessary to understand how place-based communities work to retain control in the face of powerful international processes, and to investigate attempts to use tourism as a strategy for strengthening rather than weakening the local. As discussed above, early treatments of the social and cultural aspects of tourism were skewed by the view that the 'hosts' of tourism are pre-modern, primitive, poor and technologically backward, and their (Western) 'guests' are modern, sophisticated, wealthy and technologically advanced. However, this binary classification has gradually come to be regarded as simplistic and many authors now argue that local communities – the 'hosts' of tourism – in developing nations are looking beyond the blights of mass tourism to focus on the possible benefits of smaller scaled, community-based tourism projects and the conditions that are conducive to them (Aramberri, 2001; Chan, 2006; Cole, 2007; Mbaiwa, 2004; Meethan, 2001; Milne and Ateljevic, 2001; Sherlock, 2001; van der Duim et al., 2005; Wearing and McDonald, 2002).

This chapter seeks to examine the tracks of these alternative approaches to tourism, which operate to reposition the relationship between local cultures and global tourism, and between tourists and local communities. To this end, the chapter begins by exploring what is meant by a 'social value' in the context of tourism, suggesting that such tourism initiatives (whether formal or informal) seek to endorse local peoples and cultures and to create a space within which local communities have a central role in the planning and management of tourism. The chapter then goes on to discuss backpacking as a new form of global travel. We suggest that although backpacking is global in its scope, it has emerged in ideological opposition to mass tourism as a set of practices focused on experiences of and encounters with 'authentic' local people, places and cultures. Finally, the chapter considers the repositioning of community-based approaches to tourism in developing nations to empower local populations. Case studies are drawn upon, and a model for community-based tourism is discussed. First, though, it is necessary to discuss the intersection between local communities and global tourism.

Valuing the Local

In Chapter 4 we outlined some of the conditions necessary to move locals and tourists beyond the hegemonic construction of tourism and the tourist space, particularly in developing countries. These conditions place a 'value' on the local peoples and cultures. They ensure that local communities are actively involved in tourism planning and have control over the products that comprise the tourism experience (Hay, 1988). Central to this process are the connections between local cultures and communities and the spaces of tourism. Social valuing in the context of tourism represents a physical, mental and spiritual attachment to place that is 'appropriated' into the daily lives of the people who live there:

> Our surroundings are more than their physical form. ... Places can be the embodiments of our ideas and ideals. We attach meanings to places – meanings known to individuals and meanings shared by communities. (Australian Heritage Commission, 1992: iii)

Places are conceived by local communities as having character, identity and spirit as well as meaning. Individual and collective experiences are informed by an engagement with place, and in turn these experiences create and add to the ongoing meaning of the place. In other words, place is imbued with social as well as individual value because it provides the context within which cultural practices occur and embodies cultural traditions (past), cultural identities (present) and cultural aspirations (future) (Australian Heritage Commission, 1992). The creation of social value is dependent on the existence of a dynamic relationship between those who visit a space and those for whom it is home (see, for example, Taylor, 2001). By interacting and engaging with the local community for whom the tourist destination is 'home' or a 'way of life', tourists as *chorasters* may be able to find specificity and uniqueness in local cultures, thus locating a shared, dynamic and dialogic meaning. Tourist destinations are the spaces and places within which hosts and guests interact in particular ways over a bounded period of time. In this way, and through the associated activities and rituals, the space acquires cultural meanings which are further tied to the identities of the community and the individual selves of its members.

A social-valuing approach to tourism seeks to encapsulate these ideas in tourist space by acknowledging the significance of those social processes and interactions that occur between hosts and guests and which give value to the space through the 'practice' of place. The 'social' in social valuing acknowledges that it is dependent on a dynamic relationship existing between those who use it and the shared sense of identity it provides to a community. The potential for social valuing in tourism lies in its ability to be communicated among the local community and to the tourist market more broadly. Social valuing, then, is to participate in a shared sense of meaning creating the possibility for a transformation of local and tourist. Table 6.1 outlines nine elements that have been said to comprise the social valuing of place in the context of tourism.

The experiential worth that is derived from an engagement with the past, present and imagined future of a place and its representation sets the scene for its social worth. Its maintenance and the continued interaction of people with, and in, place ensures the persistence of its social and, hence, cultural value. For example, Jensen (1998) speaks of the interaction between tourists and performers at the annual country music festival in Nashville, Tennessee. The tourism experience, it is argued, is derived from situated activities within the specific place of the event and the overall (performative) space of the town. The town takes on a set of meanings for the visitor through his/her participation in activities, exposure to local place-based knowledge, and interaction with the geo-politically defined and culturally situated place called 'Nashville'. In another

Table 6.1 Social value and the tourist space

Concept	Description
Spiritual and traditional connection	Provides spiritual or traditional connection between past and present. Ties the past and present affectionately together
Empowerment	Helps give a disempowered group back its history
Identity	Provides an essential reference point in the community's identity or sense of itself (or historical grounding)
Important reference point	Looms large in the daily comings and goings of life
Transcends use value	Provides an essential community function which over time develops into a deeper attachment that has more than just utility value
Place–human interaction	Has shaped some aspect of community behaviours or attitudes
Meaningful	Is distinctive architecturally or otherwise, to which special meanings have been attached
Regular contact	Is accessible to the public and offers the possibility of repeated use to build up ssociations and avalue to the community of users
Civic centre	Where people gather and act as a community, for example, places of public ritual, public meeting or congregation, and informal gathering places

Source: Adapted from the Australian Heritage Commission (1992: 7). *What is Social Value? A Discussion Chapter*, Technical Publications Series Number 3, copyright Commonwealth of Australia, reproduced by permission.

example, Cunningham (2006) argues that social valuing of the visited place can both enhance the tourist experience and enrich the culture and identity of the local population. He presents a case study of the Japanese island of Ogasawara, where local cultures and heritage are greatly undervalued by tourists and the tourism industry in general. In order to reverse this trend, Cunningham suggests that the 'Obeikei' community should communicate to visitors their unique understanding of, and value for, the place that is the island – its natural resources, remoteness and rich cultural history. Cunningham suggests that the local community should find a way of describing and representing their unique identity as 'islanders' to the tourists. By being exposed to messages of local value, the argument is that tourists might then be able to engage with the island's history at the invitation of the locals and on their terms. The result would be a broadening of the tourism experience of both the host and the guest. The hosts might find that their culture and local identity are affirmed, while the traveller would have a meaningful experience. As

Taylor (2001: 16) notes, 'important local values' are promoted through tourist–local interaction, communication and engagement with the local.

When locals have a voice they can communicate the social value of their place. In other words, messages can be presented to tourists that provide an important point of interest and empathy for local communities (Cole, 2007). However, in many instances, because locals are often positioned by the tourism industry as being at the bottom of the tourism hierarchy, meaningful interaction between them and tourists is difficult. The tourism experience is thus lessened as a result, particularly when the tourists seek engagement with the local. If communities are motivated and supported to represent their position in the tourism hierarchy as significant, then there is potential for them to identify, clarify and advocate their valuing of place and, subsequently, for tourists to experience the place and the way of life of local cultures. It may seem a somewhat idealistic position, but there is some evidence to suggest that social valuing can communicate spiritual or traditional connections between the past and the present with the potential for empowering currently disempowered groups by allowing them to reclaim elements of their place and culture. For example, it has been suggested that 'township tourism' in Soweto, South Africa, has instilled local residents with pride as they have been able to communicate and share their struggle with visitors, the experience of their past oppression, and their vision for freedom and economic equality in the present and the future (Cole, 2006). This may be an overstatement (and is a stark contrast to slum-and-ghetto tourism which, when run by outsiders, can operate to further objectify locals), but this example nevertheless points to an important set of tourism relationships and potential outcomes.

In recent years, therefore, the social valuing of place has gone some way towards challenging hegemonic constructions of the tourist space. This is further evidenced with reference to the renaming of (what are now) national parks, wilderness areas and territories around the world with their original indigenous names. As an outcome of eighteenth-, nineteenth- and twentieth-century Western military, political and economic dominance, many of the world's most iconic places came to be named after (colonizing) Western political leaders, monarchs, surveyors, or Western geographical designations. Examples of places recently reinstated with those names bequeathed to them by their traditional indigenous landowners include Uluṟu and Kata Tjuṯa (Ayers Rock and Mt Olga, Australia), Sagarmatha/Qomolangma (Mount Everest, Nepal and Tibet), Denali

(Mount McKinley, United States) and Nunavut (Northwest Territories, Canada). This renaming acknowledges the existence and valuing of these places prior to their 'discovery' by Western explorers and recognizes the living cultures and ways of life of the original inhabitants (Young, 2009b). As a result, contemporary links are made between the indigenous culture and particular sites, as well as a recognition of the legitimacy of indigenous place names. Thus, certain places are communicated as being associated with the culture and spiritual traditions of indigenous people. In some cases, for instance Uluru–Kata Tjuta, the renaming has been used as a symbolic gesture in the devolution of ownership and management to the traditional landowners, thus empowering them to take some level of control concerning its future (Young, 2009b).

Indigenous place names are just one aspect of social valuing that can be communicated to tourists. However, the large majority of destination images portrayed in tourism marketing materials are constructed without the participation of the local communities, who in turn have the potential to confer social value (Cunningham, 2006; Macleod, 2006). Often images do not match the tourist experience because the voices of the local people have been silenced. Social valuing recognizes that local communities hold extensive knowledge about places and an exposure to this knowledge can play a key role in the tourist experience, provided of course that the locals are in control of the interpretation and transmission of this knowledge. It can enable the tourist to transcend the Otherness implied and represented in many tourism marketing images. The involvement of local communities in the marketing of their cultures allows for a greater range and diversity of images, messages and symbols to be communicated. Locals thus determine the 'identity' of their place.

The challenge, of course, is to move beyond platitudes and statements of intent to achieve positive outcomes at the local level. Tourism generally is unplanned and disorganized. A social-valuing approach to tourism requires all levels of government, non-government organizations and locals working together to achieve sustainable outcomes that focus on the wishes of the community. If tourism is produced and distributed at the local level by local communities, it has a much greater chance of resisting the global imperatives of capital intensification (MacCannell, 2001; Ritzer, 2006; Sofield, 2003; Yudice, 1995). Indeed, in developing countries the involvement of government planners in tourism is seen as crucial for building and mediating local social value, particularly when external developers and investors are involved (Sofield, 2003; Wilson, 1997). Sofield points to the example of the collapse of a tourism resort on Anuha in the Solomon Islands when the central government failed to act in a dispute between the local community and the new owners of an existing resort who wanted to expand without local consultation.

When a breakdown in the relationship between local communities, tourism brokers and tourists occurs, the result is often conflict and the tourism industry may 'peak, fade and self destruct' (Haywood, 1988: 105). Conflicts between locals and tourists typically result from the capital intensification and economic development of a destination, which is viewed as a vehicle that will disrupt and dilute local culture (Robinson, 1999). Conflict is also likely to arise over the use of scarce resources for tourism, when locals are denied access to the natural resources upon which they base their livelihoods. Tourists may also 'display ignorance ... or ... disregard for the environment and indulge in inappropriate [and culturally insensitive] behaviour' that angers (and disempowers) the local community (Holden, 2000: 74). For example, the onset of large-scale tourism in Goa on the Western coast of India has produced pressures on both society and the environment (Brammer et al., 2004). Reactions to this increase in tourism have been varied, but organized forms of stakeholder resistance have become common. Major issues that have emerged include the community's reaction to disputes over the use of land and, in particular, the use (and abuse) of beaches by tourists and tourism operators. Conflict in Goa is centred on the main stakeholders – the small-scale entrepreneurs who seek to make a living from tourism through running beach shacks, hawking goods and organizing rave parties, and the large corporate interests whose developments include beach-front hotels and casinos, and who see the market as an unsophisticated extension of 'sun lust' tourism by Europeans. Brammer et al. (2004) argue that these and other conflicts stem largely from a lack of adequate planning, consultation and mediation between the various stakeholders by the Goan authorities – a failure to value the place and its cultures.

Alternative forms of tourism – produced by operators who are more mission-driven and ethical, and less commercialized – have sought to consider input from local communities. Often, they base their operations on a two-way interactive process between the local community and the tourist, whereby the local community and the visitor have opportunities to access different space–place dimensions from those available in conventional profit-driven modes of tourism. For example, One World Travel (OWT), owned and operated by Community Aid Abroad, redirects all profits from its trading back into local communities (Wearing, 2001). Tourists may be attracted to, and may identify with, what they see as a more ethical approach to tourism. Tourists may also be attracted by what they see as a more local, and hence authentic, tourism experience. OWT operates as a travel agency but offers a range of special 'Travel Wise' tours. The guiding principles of this organization relate to understanding the culture visited, and to respect, and be sensitive to, the people who are hosting the visit, while treading carefully on the surrounding natural environment.

Kelly (1997) conducted a study of OWT Travel Wise tours and found them to be an effective model for community-based tourism. He based this assessment on the ability of OWT tours to act as a sensitive and effective form of development, at the same time as providing the tourists with satisfying and meaningful interactions with the locals. However, he found that this type of tour is attractive to a relatively narrow segment of the population, in this case one that is predominantly female and highly educated. Kelly (1997: 49) notes that the 'OWT approach in encouraging people to travel responsibly is effective largely because the organization and its tour products attract people who have, or are inclined towards, the desired attitudes'. Therefore, it is likely to be much more difficult to apply this model to the mass tourism market, which attracts tourists with a different mix of motivations and attitudes. To counter this problem in the mass tourism market Kelly recommends that tourism brokers adopt a macro-marketing approach that:

> involves a concern with the wider social and physical environment as well as a switch from the usual emphasis on meeting customer needs to recognition that, especially in tourism, there are other stakeholders. An organization is likely to benefit from favourable publicity attracted by such a socially responsible approach. (1997: 50)

Kelly (1997) indicates that such an alternative model of tourism depends upon a considerable shift in power between Western globalizing and local developing nation communities. He argues, therefore, that an important component in this shift is the social valuing of place, which suggests meaningful representations of culture and identity as it allows both hosts and guests to move beyond oppressive or detached interactions to self-enhancing and engaging ones. This shift involves a focus on the experiential micro-politics of tourism. Face-to-face interactions between locals and tourists assume the existence of a plurality of spaces and places in which to challenge and negotiate the construction of culturally specific discourses of the social, the personal and the cultural. Ultimately, a two-way process that involves tourists 'giving something back' to the toured communities can play a key role in facilitating tourist–local interactions.

Backpackers and Global Wanderers

Experiencing the local through meeting local people and engaging with the cultures of destinations is an important travel motivation for contemporary global wanderers, popularly known as backpackers. At any given time, hundreds of thousands of young people travel the world for extended periods of time, temporarily foregoing employment or further formal education. As backpackers undertake lengthy journeys, they can incorporate a range of activities into their travel experiences, and they typically have a variety of motivations for travel. For many, in addition to seeking elements of pleasure, experiencing local lifestyles, places and cultural differences (including giving something back to the visited communities) is often considered paramount. Lengthy periods abroad with independent and flexible itineraries seemingly provide backpackers with greater opportunities to immerse themselves in destination cultures. They reportedly travel more widely than other tourists (Scheyvens, 2002), and are less interested in sightseeing than they are in experiencing, participating and learning (Loker, 1993; Loker-Murphy and Pearce, 1995). Therefore, backpacking is often considered more as a rite of passage to a worldly identity than as merely a form of diversionary leisure and recreation; it is a 'secular rite of passage that assists in the development of reflexive and potentially cosmopolitan youth identities' (Matthews, 2008b: 175). In this sense, long-term independent travel is viewed as a pursuit of self-enhancement through the accumulation of experience (Desforges, 2000).

The conceptual origins of the study of backpacking commenced with Cohen's (1972, 1973, 1974) ideas about tourist typologies, which he based on distinctions between institutionalized and non-institutionalized travellers (see Chapter 2 of this volume). Long-term independent travellers have been defined in a number of different ways, and labelled with a variety of terms, including drifters (Cohen, 1972, 1973), nomads (Cohen, 1973), youthful travellers (Teas, 1974), wanderers (Vogt, 1976), tramping youth (Adler, 1985), long-term budget travellers (Riley, 1988) and non-package Western tourists (Edensor, 1998). Over the past decade, however, long-term independent travellers have increasingly been discussed under the label of 'backpackers'. Regardless of the title that is applied, a consistent thread uniting each of the studies into this specific tourism phenomenon is the view that long-term travel provides a transitional period – an interval between everyday routine and a break from decisions regarding new or different roles and responsibilities (such as careers and marriage). These travellers are understood as being predominantly young, middle-class and well educated, and have been described as belonging to the 'new middle classes' (Mowforth and Munt, 1998; Munt, 1994). Most importantly, though, a commonly held view is that youth travellers are at a life juncture when they embark on their journeys (Cohen, 1973; Graburn, 1983; Riley, 1988; Vogt, 1976) and, in this sense, travel can be said to present young people with opportunities for personal growth and development. Travel can be a way of demonstrating independence and, as a result of their experiences and interactions with travelled places, people and cultures, backpackers can emerge from their travels feeling more knowledgeable and 'worldly'.

Richards and Wilson (2004: 10) recently noted that 'the backpacking phenomenon has developed considerably over the past thirty years, progressing from a marginal activity of a handful of "drifters" to a major global industry'. Indeed, backpacking has in many ways become an increasingly conventional and institutionalized alternative to mass tourism (Young, 2009a). The increased recognition of the significance of backpacker travellers and the rise in the number of people backpacking has resulted in an intensification of research into this type of travel as a social practice. A focus has been directed towards the diverse aspects of the backpacker phenomenon that reflect its economic, social and cultural significance and, furthermore, its status as evidence of extensive structural shifts supposedly characteristic of the transition to late (or post-) modernity. Recent studies exploring the relationship between backpacking as a travel lifestyle and as an expression of identity have found that 'backpackers often see their travels as a form of self-development, in which they learn about themselves, their own society and other cultures' (Richards and Wilson, 2004: 6). This point is summed up by Matthews:

> [D]uring one's travels, interactions with others (and, in particular, interactions with locals) may inspire greater appreciation of the world, its people and cultures. ... [W]hen such an understanding

or knowledge is attained in a personally meaningful manner, it has lasting impact for the individuals involved, rendering them in some way changed or transformed. (2008a: 101)

Similarly, Desforges (1998: 191) suggests that travel for 'white middle-class youth' is a means of constructing individual and collective identities. In particular, he emphasizes travel as a means of accumulating experiential knowledge – the 'opportunity of gaining knowledge which contrasts with the difficulties of formal education' (Desforges, 1998: 178). The educational experiences that comprise this form of knowledge are based around seeking different situations and experiences from those with which young people are familiar. According to Desforges (1998), travel provides substantial opportunities for 'collecting' places and for accumulating these desired experiences of difference. Moreover, experiences of difference provide a greater range and diversity of 'building blocks' that can serve as component elements in processes of identity formation. Elsrud (2001) also describes the travel experience as a process of narrating self-identity. Similarly, she suggests that backpacker travel experiences are primarily based on difference and Otherness:

> The more different a culture is experienced as being, the more is felt to be at stake in each situation of interaction … novelty is not enough to turn a journey into an adventure. It requires difference as well … a comparable 'Other', an 'other' quality, an 'other' being, an 'other' state of mind, upon which the adventure narrative must build its foundation. (Elsrud, 2001: 606)

Consequently, the authenticity of places and people is prominent, and a central aspect of backpacking is a search for cultural knowledge and 'contact with the authentic Other' (Phipps, 1999: 84; Young 2005). The 'authentic' encounter with the Other forms the basis for the development of experiential knowledge – of 'cultural capital' which is accumulated in the articulation and narration of self-identity, becoming a resource for obtaining and expressing social position (Bourdieu, 1984; Desforges, 1998, 2000; Elsrud, 2001; Munt, 1994). Yet, as Desforges (1998) points out, exercising cultural capital is by no means straightforward. Just because some young travellers may see their overseas journeys as a means of developing a positive self and social identity doesn't mean it will be received in the same light by those at home. Individual backpackers embark on their journeys for a diverse range of reasons and attach various meanings to their experiences. Backpackers seek out many different types of experience during their travels and their motivation for certain types of experience can transform in a single trip (Uriely et al., 2002). However, despite the specific motivations for travel, backpacking can be simultaneously considered as educational and character building, and 'is imagined as providing for the accumulation of experience, which is used to renarrate and represent self-identity' (Desforges, 2000: 942).

These above-mentioned characteristics of backpacking – a desire for interaction with others, the seeking of experiences of difference, underpinned by a search for existential authenticity – frame and shape a type of experience that encourages particular forms of social valuing and engagement and interaction with local cultures. For this reason, backpackers can be considered as alternative tourists (Young, 2008) and, perhaps more specifically, as alternative cultural tourists:

> [M]any cultural tourists (especially backpackers) will often take great delight in being sandwiched between locals and their sacks of rice or grain, or their entourage of goats or chickens. Most cultural tourists are likely to be on some kind of quest for authenticity, either in terms of self-improvement or in terms of the sites, communities and activities that they engage with or in. (Smith, 2003: 35)

The desire to experience the unique and the authentic in the local means that many backpackers will attempt to move beyond superficial experiences of place and culture. Further, as many backpackers are globally aware and knowledgeable about the effects of tourism on local cultures, they will often seek experiences that are culturally responsible and environmentally sensitive. According to Mowforth and Munt (1998: 155), the backpacker desire to pursue alternative tourism signals 'a cultural and social reaction of the new middle classes to the crassness which they perceive in tourism'. Backpackers are, therefore, often the pursuers of the various tourism alternatives that have developed to counter the negative social, cultural, economic and environmental aspects associated with mass tourism.

Volunteer tourism, for example, provides backpackers with a way to engage with local cultures at the same time as staying at a destination for an extended period (Matthews, 2008a; Young, 2008). According to Matthews (2008a: 115), backpacker involvement in volunteer tourism is about experiencing Otherness, but it also allows 'for the accumulation of experiential knowledge and personal transformation'. The notion that volunteer tourism provides a means for 'giving something back' to local communities is tempered by the fact that backpackers also gain something – in terms of knowledge and identity articulation – through their experiences. Hence, 'these simultaneous expectations foster the discourse of mutual benefit common to alternative tourism and … this discourse may assist in reinstating a sense of equality between locals and travellers' (Matthews, 2008a: 115). Indeed, various forms of volunteer tourism constitute a burgeoning area in the alternative tourism sector, and a number of case studies in a recent edited collection by Lyons and Wearing (2008) outline many of the key debates that underpin contemporary volunteer tourism, in particular the various political dimensions evident in various cultural contexts, including power, empowerment and equity (McGhee and Andereck, 2008; Raymond, 2008; Ruhanen et al., 2008; Spencer, 2008).

In the context of community- (or place-) based tourism discussed in this chapter, the discourse of mutual benefit is, of course, significant. As backpackers engage in alternative forms of tourism, such as cultural tourism and volunteer tourism, the tourist destination becomes 'an interactive space where tourists become creative actors who engage in behaviours that are mutually beneficial to host communities, and to the cultural and social environments of those communities' (Lyons and Wearing, 2008: 6). The local–global interactions common to these forms of tourism have been found to have a positive impact on local community development in destinations in both non-Western and Western countries (see, for example, Scheyvens, 2002; Westerhausen and Macbeth, 2003). There is, however, a need to approach any such tourism development with a level of caution, and because a key focus of tourism is authenticity, there is a potential for backpackers to hold idealized expectations of everyday visited places and cultures which can lead to tensions between host and guest. Further, a desire for 'meaningful' and 'real' experiences can draw attention away from the often constructed nature of the 'authentic' (Smith, 2003; see also Bruner, 1991).

Backpackers can and do provide significant benefits to local communities, particularly in terms of local development. Similarly, studies of backpacking can provide valuable insights into the construction of the traveller self and the social valuing of place. Scheyvens (2002), in her study of backpackers and development in the Third World, found that for local communities that wish to be involved in tourism, the backpacker market can benefit them in an equitable and mutually beneficial way. Local communities can maintain ownership and control of tourism resources, and they 'can provide services and products demanded by these tourists without the need for large amounts of start-up capital or sophisticated infrastructure, and they can retain control over such enterprises' (Scheyvens, 2002: 157). They can also control the stories, histories and place identities that they value. The tourist destination can therefore be an interactive space where local communities are empowered through community-based tourism. Thus, as backpackers search for authenticity – primarily objective and existential (Wang, 1999, 2000; see Chapter 2 of this volume) – in their encounters with local communities and places, it is possible that they may be 'natural allies in local communities' struggle to maintain their identity and preserve their social and cultural environment' (Westerhausen and Macbeth, 2003: 75). Arguably, community-based tourism ventures that attract backpackers and other alternative tourists have significant potential to provide a more sustainable approach to community-based tourism development.

Hybrid Travel Cultures

Milne and Ateljevic (2001: 374) argue that community-based approaches to tourism are becoming central to many tourism development plans around the world, particularly in developing nations. At the same time there is a growing realization that localized cooperation, trust and networking are essential ingredients in providing the right mix for successful tourism outcomes. Cole (2007), in her study of the 'Ngadha' from the Indonesian island of Flores, found that local ownership and control of the resource base was pivotal to the success of tourism development in the area. From interviews, surveys and observations she found that locals equated modernization with electricity, education and healthcare, and that none of these things conflicted with their cultural traditions or *adat* (the way of the ancestors). Local Indonesian officials charged the Ngadha with selling their culture, yet the villagers were happy to commodify their dance displays, believing that it was not possible to sell *adat* ceremonies. Cole adds:

> The villagers of Ngadha like tourists for a number of reasons: they provide entertainment, bring economic benefits and service provision, provide friends from faraway places, and are a source of information. Importantly, they make the locals proud of their cultural heritage. ... The cultural commodification of their difference has led to a recognizable 'ethnic group' identity. This process of commodification of the villagers' identity is bringing

them pride and a self-conscious awareness of their traditional culture, which has become a resource that they manipulate to economic and political ends. (2007: 955)

The view is that if small local tourism developments are to succeed then communities need to be seen not as fixed entities, collections of self-contained essential characteristics, or as passive 'victims' of global development, but as dynamic interacting systems whose cultures and ways of life are capable of adaptation and cultural and economic sustainability (Meethan, 2001; Sofield, 2003). If we approach locally-based tourism as a complex and sometimes fluid notion, then the interactive space between tourist and local communities comes to be viewed as a continuous process whereby different social practices and values meet and new meanings are created (Wearing and McDonald, 2002). The division of power between and within communities, tourism entrepreneurs, intermediary organizations and the tourists themselves is then highlighted in the process of tourism planning and development. Mowforth and Munt (2003) suggest that with respect to tourism development in local communities, possibilities for positive change are unlikely to come from the international, national or regional levels where the power of vested interests is too great. Instead, they are more likely to come from below, at the local (village) level, where the need for and acknowledgment of change are greatest. This idea sits within the framework of inclusiveness, where, historically, communities in developing countries have been written out of tourism planning, whereas now they are seen as a central part of the development process (Cole, 2006, 2007; Sofield, 2003; van der Duim et al., 2005; Wearing and McDonald, 2002).

The analysis of power in tourism studies has often focused on power at the macro or geopolitical level. However, in recent years there has been an increasing acknowledgement that an understanding of the power relations that exist at the local level is essential to successful tourism development and planning initiatives in developing nations. Cole (2006) argues that empowerment at the local level can be achieved through educating locals about tourists and tourism, providing access to information, skills training and capacity building. More importantly, legal and institutional change is required in order to allow for a genuine reallocation of decision-making power to the local community members themselves. Sofield (2003) acknowledges that tourism in developing nations has begun to focus on community consultation. More often than not, however, the path of development has been carried out on behalf of communities rather than development by communities. Sofield explores tourism development at various levels (national, regional and local) in the South Pacific and argues that community participation can be an important means of resisting the traditional imposition of outside organizations (multinationals, international government, national government) which often act as post-colonizers. Sofield (2003) presents three case studies to illustrate his points. The first focuses on the Solomon Islands, where the government instituted a National Tourism Policy in 1990. The policy had little effect at the local level because villagers perceived a lack of participation and control. This was the result of a continuing 'colonial legacy' and legislation that precluded local responsibility and any acknowledgement or sensitivity of cultural differences at the local level (Sofield, 2003).

In contrast, the two other case studies highlight the benefits of empowering local communities by ensuring they had responsibility and ownership of the tourism development processes (Sofield, 2003). In the first instance, a local community on the island of Vanuatu began performing important traditional events for tourists, which they were able to do by reaching a consensus among themselves and exercising control over the venture in order to protect its cultural significance. In the second instance, local community members in the Mana Island Resort in Fiji were represented on its board of directors. As a result, 'meaningful' development had taken place in the local community adjacent to the resort, and the local community had control over the natural resources of their place through a land-leasing contract, whereby any proposed expansion would require the permission of community representatives.

Table 6.2 outlines a different understanding and framework for local–tourist interactions and the exchange of cultural identity and symbols in local places. The alternate model presented here is, as an ideal type, dependent on a more equitable distribution of power between Western and local cultures, where interaction occurs in a 'third tourist space' (see Chapter 7 of this volume), decision-making responsibility involves the locals and they receive economic returns from the tourism enterprise. In this model, tourism is not exploitative of local populations and the benefits flow to local residents. The culture of the local community is thus respected and the tourist is open to experiencing aspects of the Other culture with a view to learning and expanding the tourist self.

This shift in the relationships of power between tourist cultures and local cultures enables both hosts and guests to interact and to learn from each other with an eventual hybridization of cultures. This

Table 6.2 Model for community-based cultural tourism

Concept	Western society	Local community
Power	Economic and cultural exchange; more equitable distribution of power	Economic and cultural exchange; more equitable distribution of power
Culture	Hybridization	Hybridization
Values	Quality of life – exploring new boundaries	Survival with increased standard of living, retaining cultural values
Place/space	Tourist destination a space to learn and interact with environment and culture	Spaces imbued with traditional social value but open to dynamic interaction
People	Tourists as *chorasters* looking for interaction and learning about others	Locals as educators and interpreters
Selves, 'I', 'me'	Hybridized and fluid, incorporating new aspects from 'other' cultures	Hybridized and fluid; 'I', 'you', and 'we'

Source: Wearing and Wearing (2006: 160) 'Rereading the subjugating tourist in neoliberalism: Postcolonial otherness and the tourist experience', *Tourism Analysis*, 11(2): 145–63. Reproduced with permission.

shift is also in keeping with the hybridization experienced more generally around the world as a result of globalization. Tourism and the tourist destination then become spaces for interaction and learning and do not damage or destroy the cultures and places of the host community. The tourist as *choraster* is actively involved in the representation and interpretation of local cultures and places in the context of aspects of their own culture. Locals become reflexive educators and translators. The selves of both the tourists and the locals, therefore, are able to move beyond the constraints of dominance and exploitation to experience tourism through a process of enrichment and negotiation. The hybridization of the tourist self enables a communication in which 'they' or the Other is transposed into 'you' and 'I'. Instead of hegemony, where one culture (guests) dominates and renders the other culture (hosts) inferior, there are possibilities for cultural interaction, respect and growth of the selves involved.

Conclusion

The purpose of this chapter was to explore the ways in which local communities can resist and regain control of their places and cultures in the context of global tourism. In our initial discussion, it was argued that the local–tourist relationship commonly privileges the developed over developing nations, resulting in the internalization of Western cultural values and beliefs, including those associated with commodification and individualism. This is a form of 'cultural cannibalism' (see Chapter 4), whereby the tourist culture submerges and eventually eclipses the other culture. It operates by reinforcing and homogenizing dominant Western culture. As such, there is a fixity of both local and tourist identity and little room for self-reflexivity through the experience of tourism and engagement with its spaces and cultures. The economic and, hence, representational power of tourist marketers has often enabled them to commodify and package their own interpretations of Otherness in developing countries, where tourists are encouraged to be voyeurs who glimpse aspects of the other culture, which is often dressed up to conform to the image which has been presented in glossy advertising brochures and television travel programmes. Tourist destinations are presented as places for viewing the Other rather than as spaces with which and within which to interact.

In order to move beyond the hegemonic construction of tourist space, we suggested in this chapter that smaller-scaled, community-based tourism has the potential to provide a more sustainable approach. A review of recent research here suggests that conditions which enable this to occur include localized cooperation, ownership of the resource base, acknowledging the adaptation capabilities of local communities, capacity-building in the form of education, the investment and reallocation of decision-making power and responsibility to the local level, a local desire to participate, and the need for cultural understanding and respect for difference and diversity at all levels of government. From these conditions we presented a more inclusive model of cultural tourism, which places a social value on the local meaning of place. Backpacking is a contemporary form of travel that is framed around social valuing and, ideally, the sharing and exchange of cultures. Through the spaces of travel, the power balance between tourist and hosts can thus be destabilized and the cultural hegemony can be challenged. As travel and tourism become increasingly global and, with this globalization, attention turns to issues of hybridity and the spatialized local, there has been an associated increase in the importance of understanding the role of other forms of space in the process. Increasingly, the travel experience is mediated by the spaces of representation and imagination, and it is to a consideration of these issues that attention will now turn.

7

Tourism, Space and Representation

Within the study of tourism, space and place are increasingly being recognized as socio-cultural constructions rather than simply physical locations or destinations. As such, tourist space can be viewed as a site through which 'power, identity, meaning and behaviour are constructed, negotiated and renegotiated according to socio-cultural dynamics' (Aitchison and Reeves, 1998: 51). The engagement with space is also central to the shaping of the traveller self. The recognition that space has both material and symbolic dimensions is important in providing the framework for reconceptualizing tourist cultures in terms of the interplay between the travel space and the travel experience. Space and travel are both real and imagined. In this context, this chapter considers the significance of virtual tourist space and mediated tourism experiences to an understanding of the tourist experience and the traveller self. Pivotal here again are notions of authenticity and the virtual. With its emphasis on experience in the absence of 'being there' and co-presence, some have suggested that virtual tourism may well present one solution to the issues of climate change and sustainability that currently confront the tourism industry.

In this chapter we argue that the traveller self is mediated as much through the spaces of representation and imagination as it is through 'real' encounters and a co-presence in 'real' tourist space. It removes the emphasis from the staging of the site (and images of the site, in the form of postcards, posters, souvenirs, brochures and websites) and places it on how the tourist experiences the site. Thus an 'existential' understanding of authenticity can provide a more fruitful approach from which to theorize the tourist experience. In understanding the traveller self as one who engages fully with the travel experience, we suggest that destination imaging and imagery support a multiplicity of perspectives and engagements with place and experience. The chapter begins by examining the role that images can play in shaping the tourism destination and the traveller self. Images are both private, in the sense of being personal photographs that serve as markers of having been there, as well as public. They are about the individual and the collective. The chapter goes on to discuss the ways in which the travel experience is increasingly constituted through the texts of the image and the written word. This merging is most evident through the use of the internet and other forms of communications technologies, which are sometimes regarded as markers of post-tourism. Finally, the chapter introduces the notion of thirdspace as a way of highlighting the multiplicity of perspectives that may be incorporated into the spaces of the traveller self and of moving beyond the dichotomies that continue to be a feature of tourism studies.

Image, Memory and Imagination

The popularity of photographing tourist landscapes, in order either to possess them or make them desirable to friends, family and work colleagues, is an important aspect of contemporary tourist cultures and the imagining of the traveller self. Indeed, in some contexts, images of the tourist space (and of the people encountered in this space) can sometimes become more important than the travel experience itself (Dann, 1993). Photographs can come to stand for the real – they are triggers for memory and imagination, central elements of the travel narrative. As Jamieson (1962) points out, the American tourist no longer lets the landscape 'be in its being', but takes a photograph of it. The space and experience are thus transformed into both object and sign. Bennett notes:

> The concrete activity of looking at a landscape – including, no doubt, the disquieting bewilderment with the activity itself, the anxiety that must arise when human beings, confronting the non-human, wonder what they are doing there and what the point or purpose of such a confrontation might be in the first place – is thus comfortably replaced by the act of taking possession of it and converting it into a form of personal property. (1998: 17)

Crawshaw and Urry (1997) regard photography as an important aspect of contemporary tourism and the tourist gaze. They point out that the emergence of mass tourism actually coincided with the development of photography and, as a result, photography was from the outset a central aspect of the social construction of tourism. They go on to suggest that because of these intersections, photography has become part of the 'language by which we learn to describe and appreciate the environment' (1997: 183) and the visual has developed as central to the construction of traveller memories. Photography and the image are therefore also central to the formation of the traveller self. Crawshaw and Urry explain the travel/photography nexus as follows:

> It is the visual images of places that give shape and meaning to the anticipation, experience and memories of travelling. ... Photographs provide evidence – that you have been away, that the mountains were that high, that the weather was so good. At home, afterwards, the visual images are interwoven with the verbal commentary to remember the experience and to tell others about it. (1997: 179)

For Crawshaw and Urry, the significance of photography in shaping contemporary tourism goes beyond the personal photographs of individual pleasure travellers. Rather, they are interested in particular in the ways in which what they term 'public photography' frames dominant understandings and expectations of specific holiday destinations, as well as holiday behaviour and experiences. The images which appear in place-marketing texts, including travel brochures, postcards and official travel guides as public photographs, are important in the construction of tourism. As Crawshaw and Urry (1997: 194) describe it, 'the travel photographer and the tourist seem to engage in a mutually reinforcing social process of constructing and altering images of places and experiences'. In this respect, the image has both a symbolic and a material form – it operates simultaneously 'as mirror, as ritual, as language, as dominant ideology, and as resistance' (Crawshaw and Urry, 1997: 184).

Much of the tourism literature to date has been concerned with the 'authenticity' or otherwise of people, objects and places in the cultural tourist's view, including the representation of this 'reality' in tourism marketing. As we discussed in Chapter 3, tourists consistently ask whether what they are seeing is 'the real thing'. They want to be assured of the authenticity of the costumes, dance, music, food, décor and artefacts that they come into contact with as the markers of destination cultures. However, as we have argued here, the social and environmental interaction that the tourist creates in tourist space also

constitutes the experience as 'authentic' in the sense of being meaningful, along with the images, landscapes and artefacts. It is this aspect
of travel that has the ability to contribute to an expanded and enhanced
sense of the traveller self. Such experiences, together with their impacts
on the self, rather than what is viewed, are what the tourist takes home
and 'sees' in, and remembers from, the travel images that document
the trip. Images, both those consumed prior to travelling and those
collected while on the road, are important aspects of this process
of forming the traveller self, but the experience cannot be reduced
to them.

Jenkins' (2003) notion of a 'circle of representation' is useful here in
that it provides further insights into the way in which images/
photographs can contribute to the construction of the tourist reality.
Jenkins suggests that as images taken by professional photographers
or other image-makers (at the behest of organizations marketing
tourism destinations or products) are promoted to particular markets,
they come to be perceived as 'real' images of the destination. As real
images they are then often replicated in the personal photography of
tourists (Jenkins, 2003). The official image marks a 'site' as a 'sight'
(Culler, 1981), which is in turn 'captured' or claimed by the tourist
through the act of replicating the photograph. The resulting image
then becomes a marker for both the place and the experience, the visual
evidence of having 'been there'. This outcome, it is suggested by Jenkins,
is the production of a singular perspective that dominates the framing
of tourism images, and thus shapes tourist perceptions of the 'real' or
'authentic' and the visitable. In other words, following Culler (1981),
the tourist seeks to see/visit what has been represented, they judge the
place or experience as authentic with reference to the official image, and
then as a marker of their visit to, and experience of, the place they will
frequently take their own photograph of the site that mirrors the official
photograph.

Through the circle of representation and the intersection of public
and private travel photography, images operate at both the level of the
individual and of the collective/social. According to Jenkins:

> ... tourist destination images are conceived as operating
> both at a *collective* level where many people within a culture
> may share particular aspects of an image, and at an *individual*
> level whereby an individual person may hold both stereotypical
> and idiosyncratic ideas about a particular tourist destination.
> (2000: n.p.)

The recognition of the collective nature of tourist destination images, which was largely unexplored prior to the above research, holds promise for the incorporation of marginalized views into what are ultimately constructed and promoted as destination images. There is significant potential, consistent with the theme of reconceptualizing the traveller in terms of the experiencing *choraster*, towards developing a framework for understanding destination imaging whereby the multiplicity of perspectives are incorporated into images. This recognition might, in turn, have positive implications not only for visitor perceptions, but also for their experiences, as well as for many local tourism stakeholders.

Contemporary tourism and the traveller self may well be framed through photography both still and moving, individual and collective. But as discussed in Chapter 3, before photography there was the written word, and travel experiences continue to be expressed, explained and constructed in a range of written travel texts, from journals and diaries, through to monographs and, more recently, email, weblogs and online interactive social spaces, such as Facebook (www.facebook.com) and MySpace (www.myspace.com). Indeed, Facebook and MySpace are particularly interesting as they make it possible for the traveller to reflect immediately on the travel experience, usually through a combination of text, image and interpretation, and through these reflections to interact while in the material travel space, with both travelling and non-travelling others. These spaces and technologies are thus reconfiguring the relationship between home and away that is at the heart of travel and the travel experience. As White and White (2007: 89) put it, the traveller can now 'be socially present while physically absent'. New communications technologies can thus disrupt the established notions of place and time that frame dominant understandings of travel as the travel destination and traveller experience come to be filtered/mediated through the ongoing engagement during travel with home and the familiar.

Texts – words and pictures – construct the tourist gaze and the travel experience. They interpret and represent the traveller and their travels for a particular readership/viewer. And in so doing the personal becomes the (quasi)public. Travel texts can thus provide rich insights into the ways in which discourse is used to frame imaginings of the self, place and Other within tourism (Johnson, 2006). There have been suggestions too that travel writing has the ability to contribute to what is termed global literacy. From her study of women's writings about their travels to the Islamic Republic of Iran, Johnson (2006) is sceptical about how much travel writing can meaningfully contribute to global literacy. She argues that the traveller texts she analysed revealed much more about the traveller self and the cultures and societies from which the traveller came, than they did about the travelled spaces and cultures. Johnson further claims that: 'these writings appear in context and the authors of such texts craft discourse to construct sociocultural imaginings of the self and Other – of a journey told from a particular viewpoint, in a particular time, to a particular audience' (2006: v).

If, following Sontag (1979), 'photography is the contemporary form taken by *flânerie*' (Crawshaw and Urry, 1997: 194), then it is possible that in the merging of the image and the script – the photograph and the reflective narrative – the traveller self becomes constituted as *choraster*. Words and images intersect in the travel discourses of cyberspace, the private and the public become indivisible as the travel experience is constructed in dialogue with the others of both home and away. The others of the travel experience are not simply those encountered in the tourist space but are the readers of the travel texts, as well as of the texts the traveller reads and consumes before, during and after travel. The importance of cyberspace to the process and experience of travel, particularly as it relates to an engagement with authenticity, has recently been explored through the lens of what is termed 'post-tourism'.

Post-Tourism and Beyond

The opposition of the terms 'tourist' and 'traveller', with its associated negative and positive connotations, continues to permeate both the tourism literature and popular impressions about which form of travel is the more socially, culturally and environmentally responsible. As we discussed in Chapter 2, notions of the traveller versus the tourist also hinge to a considerable degree on judgements regarding the extent to which different travellers and travel contexts are able to connect with the local in ways that are 'authentic', including engaging with local people and seeing and experiencing local places and forms of cultural expression. Ritzer (2000) argues, however, that it has become increasingly difficult to find travel experiences and places that are non-standardized or untouched by the tourism industry. Even those travellers, such as backpackers (see Chapter 6 of this volume), who are keen to assert their difference/distance from mainstream tourists and tourism destinations, have been shown to rely heavily on products supplied by the tourism industry. Of particular significance are guidebooks (notably, *Lonely Planet*) which are used extensively by backpackers as they plan and negotiate their journeys and travel experiences (Young, 2009a). Backpackers, even more than other travellers/tourists, are also keen users of communications technologies, in particular the internet and mobile phones, which, as argued above, are disrupting many taken-for-granted aspects of the travel process and experience which shape the traveller self.

One concept that has gained currency in trying to move the debate beyond the tourism/traveller dichotomy is that of the experientially focused 'post-tourist'. According to Feifer's original (1986) formulation, the post-tourist is mindful and good-naturedly aware of the inauthenticity of travel destinations and their travel experiences – they are 'self distanced and conscious' (Arellano, 2004: 70). For Feifer (1986), post-tourism has three key dimensions. First, the centrality of new technologies, including the internet, television and virtual reality, makes it possible for the post-tourist to 'gaze' on or 'visit' destinations without actually leaving home. Second, the highly differentiated nature of contemporary tourism means that post-tourists have far more tourism experiences and destinations to choose from than do conventional tourists. And finally, post-tourists are fully aware that there are no 'authentic' travel experiences. They are thus knowingly (and often ironically) playing a game, adopting a persona. Rojek (1993) argues that this game is one that is defined in terms of both commodification and the consumption of signs. The post-tourist is supposedly stimulated by the intertextuality of tourist spaces, that is spaces conceived by a mosaic of discourses involved in an ongoing dialogue with another, and where there is an implicit valuing of 'the experience as an end in itself' (Rojek, 1993: 177).

The idea that actual travel can be replaced with the 'virtual' is a fascinating one and, according to some commentators, virtual tourism has the potential to reshape tourism expectations and the tourist experience (Swarbrooke, 1999). At its core, this form of tourism is tourism without travel, travel without physical departure – the departure which occurs is located in the imaginary, and the destination is the space of the image/imagination rather than a geographical location. In the mix of the technologies that are redefining the tourist/post-tourist space, two are particularly noteworthy: the cyber-tourist phenomenon of online virtual/synthetic worlds, such as 'Second Life' (http://secondlife.com/), and the enveloping cinematic travel space of the IMAX screen.

In a newspaper article that canvasses whether 'cyberspace could be the next big holiday destination', Western Australian journalist Katja Gaskell (2007: n.p.) describes the following (rather appealing) scenario:

So, imagine a holiday where you begin the day with a cruise around crystal clear Caribbean waters before heading to the mountains for a spot of skiing. Later you'll watch a gig and enjoy a couple of cocktails before trying out some new dance moves at an outdoor club. Along the way you will have squeezed in some shopping, visited the Star Trek museum and paid your respects at church; the Church of Elvis that is.

Best thing about this holiday? You've only been gone three hours, didn't need a passport and the flights were free.

Gaskell's travellers may well be visiting Second Life, an online or synthetic world created in 2003 which reportedly boasts a membership in excess of 7.5 million people worldwide (Gaskell, 2007). In Second Life, the image is both the experience and the travel space. There are even specialist tour operators which run guided tours to a range of online worlds, including Second Life, and it is revealing to consider the language used by these operators to sell the travel commodities they offer. For instance, the online guided tour operator Synthravels claims there are 'many lands to discover, extraordinary places to visit, that will ravish your imagination'. It goes on to make the tantalizing promise that:

Traveling in these territories will be like dreaming: you will see exotic landscapes where among prehistoric trees break out bizarre surrealistic architectures, strange fantasy regions where the elves built astonishing temples, synthetic deserts covered with post-atomic ruins, seas of pixels where float ghostly vessels, organic architectures that conceal undercover avatars. (http://www.synthravels.com/mission/?lang=en, retrieved October 2008, original emphasis removed)

This is the language of co-presence – of being there. And yet all that is really on offer are images, or signs, of place and experience. There are now also 'real world' travel companies that have a presence in the virtual world. For example, in April 2007 STA Travel (2007) announced the opening of its Second Life operation with a press release that includes a statement by its North America Vice President of Marketing and E-commerce, Kristen Celko, that 'Students don't need a travel company to move them around in Second Life, but they do need someone to provide a "soft landing" as they enter Second Life for the first time'.

All experiences in these synthetic worlds are mediated through the persona of an avatar, which stands in for the 'real' traveller. It is the avatar 'who' has the experience. It is the avatar 'who' interacts with the destination and with the 'others' encountered in the travelled space. They are virtual travellers travelling through virtual space – the human controller remains place-based and watching. They are detached from the physicality of travelling.

While travel to synthetic worlds is mediated very directly by the image, the travel experiences packaged through the consumption of IMAX technology are rather different. IMAX experiences may be 'virtual' but the experiencing body and the physical sensations being felt are real. It is the 'traveller', not an avatar, who sits in the theatre (or wherever the screen is located) and engages with the range of sensory triggers (including the visual) that are stimulated. It is in its ability to engage the senses that the IMAX is said to approximate the 'travel' experience. Acland (1998: 430) suggests that the 'IMAX screen' can easily be mistaken for 'a wonderful, varying window on to real and imagined worlds'. The screen is overwhelming in size. It is designed to engulf the traveller/viewer in sensations of image, sound and movement. The official IMAX website describes this sensory moment as follows: 'SEE MORE, HEAR MORE, FEEL MORE – IMAX is the ultimate movie experience. With crystal clear images and wraparound digital surround sound, IMAX lets you feel like you're really there.' It goes on to promise that through IMAX the viewer will:

> Climb the daunting heights of Everest. Experience the weightlessness of space. Dive into the undersea world to see incredible creatures. Get behind the wheel of a racing car going 200mph. Travel into exciting sci/fi worlds. (http://www.imax.com/ImaxWeb/imaxExperience.do?param_section=whatImax&param_subMenuSelect=whatImaxSelect, retrieved October 2008)

The language of the promotional material is that of being there – 'viewers' are invited to 'see', 'hear', 'climb', 'experience', 'dive' and 'travel'. The key, of course, is not that they will actually be there, but that it will 'feel' as if they are. IMAX technology engages the senses in very direct ways. The physical sensations of sight, sound and movement that the IMAX traveller experiences are qualitatively different from those which might come from watching the image of an avatar visiting a destination in a virtual world. What needs to be considered therefore is the extent to which the 'almost being there' of the IMAX experience can be considered a substitute for the 'being there and getting there' of 'real' travel. In some instances it probably is the case that people who will never climb Mount Everest or go deep sea diving will be able to have some sense of what such experiences and places are like. To that extent IMAX can perhaps be a substitute for the real. But it is as an adjunct to travel that IMAX most directly intersects with the cultures of tourism. IMAX technology has the capacity to enrich the (actual) travel experience, heighten the anticipation of travelling to a particular destination, and prompt memories of having been there. It may also serve to make certain destinations seem attractive. It is this potential that is being grasped by many tourism marketers. The IMAX experience is increasingly being used to augment an already occurring physical engagement with a tourism destination; it does not stand for the sight, it enhances it. As Acland puts it: 'One does not plan a vacation around the Grand Canyon IMAX; one goes to the Grand Canyon, where the IMAX is one of the many tourist-related experiences available to sample' (1998: 437). In other words, the immersion of the IMAX can contextualize a destination, heighten expectations of 'the real' and contribute to the formation of a travel narrative. It is not, however, a substitute for travel. Rather it is both an experience in its own right and an aspect of the 'being there'. In this context, Acland (1998: 435) also discusses the use of IMAX technology in museums and other heritage sites, saying that it is 'consonant with the museum's new relations between entertainment and education'.

In addition to being situated within the realm of travel because of the ways in which it constructs and represents travel destinations and experiences, including the past, a visit to an IMAX theatre itself can also often be part of a broader tourism experience. IMAX theatres are still not particularly commonplace – Sydney, the largest city in Australia, for example, has only one such commercial cinema – and those that do exist are frequently located in the major cities. Moreover, they are usually also situated in a designated tourist precinct of these cities. This is the case in Sydney, where the IMAX cinema is at Darling Harbour, a redeveloped festival marketplace waterfront site that is very popular with both international and domestic tourists (see Chapter 5 of this volume for a discussion of waterfront tourist developments). In this way, the IMAX can often be part of a broader travel experience rather than a destination in its own right. IMAX is thus, to borrow a phrase from Sorkin (1992), a 'variation on a theme park'.

In Ross's (2005: 87) opinion, cyber-tourism is 'evolving as a response to factors such as the mercurial developments in information and communication technology, together with widespread environmental impact concerns emanating from domains such as nature-based tourism'. Ross accepts the argument that authenticity in tourism stems from the social and relational activities that flow from it, and argues that cyber-tourism has the potential to threaten these benefits. He offers a communitarian perspective by elaborating on the mechanisms whereby both bonding and bridging social networks associated with cyber-tourism may be modified and monitored for the benefit of all stakeholders. It is also the case that the new information created by virtual reality puts tourists in a position to experience something unique and relevant to themselves. Hence the experience is 'authentic' as it is (following Rojek) an 'end in itself'. Nevertheless, for most people the travel experience is considerably more than can be created by virtual reality. It also involves a direct interaction with people (hosts) as well as with spaces and images. The emotional responses that are prompted are different from those stimulated by the virtual. For example, IMAX theatre's *Everest* film feature cannot re-create the experience of climbing this mountain. But this is not a simple question of veracity or of difference in nature. The cyber is not a space apart. It is a third tourist space because the imaginary cannot be separated from the real. Where the discussion about virtual tourism and the post-tourist is most useful, therefore, is not in resolving the opposition between concepts of the traveller and the tourist. It is in expanding the conception of what is understood as travel and the travel space. Travel is about movement and immersion, but it is no longer always about geography and co-presence. It is also about the consumption of signs and imagery and the quest for experiences that do not necessarily involve physical travel. As the travel space is redefined so, too, are the traveller and notions of the traveller self.

The 'Thirdspace' of the Traveller Self

In a world that is increasingly interconnected and where more and more experiences and perceptions are mediated by signs and representations, people, whether through physical contact (migration, immigration, tourism) and/or exposure to media images and information (television, film, internet, travel guides), are aware of the practices and ways of thinking of 'others' from nations around the globe. Indeed, with respect to travel, the cultural practices and belief systems of both the traveller and the travelled are frequently, if not changed, then reinterpreted as a result of these processes of connection. Thus tourist cultures and the travel space 'cannot simply be said to belong to one discrete culture or another' (Hubbard et al., 2004: 55). Under these conditions, the static universalizing notion of traveller identity as having been formed on the basis of binary oppositions (such as between 'us' and 'them', 'self' and 'other', 'traveller' and 'tourist') also starts to break down.

As a central pivot of his influential critique of the universalizing and essentialist ways in which Western liberal democracies position 'other' cultures in order to contain and manipulate them, the postcolonial theorist Homi Bhabha (1994) introduced the concept of the 'third space'. The third space is the 'place' where identity is (re)negotiated.

> This third space involves a simultaneous coming and going in a borderland zone between different modes of action. A prerequisite for this is that we must believe that we can inhabit these different sites, making each a space of relative comfort. To do so will require inventing creative ways to cross perceived and real 'borders'. The third space is thus a place of invention and transformational encounters, a dynamic in-between space that is imbued with the traces, relays, ambivalences, ambiguities and contradictions, with the feelings and practices of both sites, to fashion something different, unexpected. (Routledge, 1996: 406)

In other words, as Meredith (1998: 2) explains, the thirdspace refers to those 'indeterminate spaces in-between subject-positions that are ... the locale of the disruption and displacement of hegemonic colonial narratives of cultural structures and practices'. The thirdspace renders ambivalent established structures of meaning and accepted points of cultural reference. It disrupts the dominant sense of history, identity and culture. The notion of the thirdspace is thus also useful in framing an expanded understanding of contemporary (post-) tourism and the traveller self. Bhabha (1994) argues that by reinterpreting the culture(s) of Western modernity through the concept of the third space, a precondition is created for the articulation of difference and diversity. Bhabha (1990) also developed the associated concept of 'hybridity' as the renegotiation of identity and a movement away from the existence of a prior, taken-for-granted culture (see

Chapter 6 of this volume). Culture and identity are formed through the hybridity of this thirdspace:

> [T]he importance of hybridity is not to be able to trace two orig-
> inal moments from which the third emerges, rather hybridity to
> me is the 'third space' which enables other positions to emerge.
> This third space displaces the histories that constitute it, and
> sets up new structures of authority, new political initiatives,
> which are inadequately understood through received wisdom.
> (Bhabha, 1990: 211)

It is the third space that makes hybridity possible. Imagining tourism and the travel experience through the lens of a third space opens up the possibility of renegotiating and repositioning the identities of the traveller self. The space becomes a site for resistance and contestation – a strategic reversal of the processes of domination whereby the gaze of the other is turned back upon the 'eye of power' (Bhabha, 1994). It also becomes a space for experimenting with, and negotiating, different forms of traveller identity. In the thirdspace, local, national and cultural identities function in the context of fluid ongoing processes – 'hybrids' – which are constructed, deconstructed and reconstructed anew. Hollinshead (1998, 2004), in his application of Bhabha's ideas to tourism, suggests that tourism and tourist destinations are important sites for cultural production and negotiation, and thus hybridity. Tourists and tourist spaces offer possibilities to resist essentialist identities and stereotypes through the performances of anonymity and through experimentation and interaction with peoples, cultures and environments that, for the tourist at least, are very different from the everyday. Media and communications technologies and the global circulation of images clearly play a pivotal role in this process.

Law (1997) provides an example of the invention of a thirdspace within tourism in his study of Filipino 'bar women', who, he says, resist the hegemonic construction of their host identity. Law (1997: 116) argues that the thirdspace here is characterized by the continual negotiation of identity, whereby these women are able to redefine the host–guest relationships to which they are subject. The interplay between the powerful (guests) and the powerless (hosts) is said to operate within a thirdspace, whereby 'identities are continuously negotiated through spaces of difference and in this way identity is constituted by encounters with otherness' (Law, 1997: 110). This conception of thirdspace implies a plurality of exchanges and interactions between the tourist and the host, which in turn reconstitutes the terms of the values and constructions that are attached to a specific and unique cultural (tourist) space. We would further suggest that post-tourist engagements with signs and simulacra are part of the processes of both negotiation and resistance.

Like Bhabha, the African-American cultural theorist bell hooks (1990) seeks to challenge what she regards as the essentialist, stable and white processes of Euro-American identity formation, which she argues have objectified black American women, forcing them to create their identities on the 'margins' of mainstream society. Having grown up in a racially segregated town in Kentucky in the 1950s, hooks experienced exclusion and marginalization firsthand. Her innovation is to use these experiences and her social location as a position (space) from which to challenge dominant social and cultural norms associated with class, gender and race.

> This is a response from the radical space of my marginality. It is a space of resistance. It is a space I choose. … This is an intervention. A message from that space in the margin that is a site of creativity and power, that inclusive space where we recover ourselves, where we move in solidarity to erase the category colonized/colonizer. Marginality as a site of resistance. Enter that space. Let us meet there. Enter that space. (hooks, 1990: 152)

hooks also employs the notion of the homespace (which equates in many respects to Bhabha's thirdspace) to reveal the processes and realities of social injustice and to generate new ways of thinking about these spaces and about the ways in which encounters which occur within them operate both to marginalize those who are 'different' and provide them with the discursive terrain that makes resistance possible.

The geographer Soja (1996) draws on the work of both hooks and Bhabha in his formulation of the notion of 'thirdspace', which he describes as 'a purposefully tentative and flexible term that attempts to capture what is actually a constantly shifting and changing milieu of ideas, events, appearance, and meanings' (Soja, 1996: 2). Soja seeks to explore the possibilities inherent in approaches that locate the margins (or borderlands) as a site of resistance and a place where new forms of subjectivity are developed. In particular, he is interested in the spatial imagination which, he argues, is implicit in hooks's conceptualization of the margins. According to Soja (1996: 12), 'hooks recomposes our lived spaces of representation as potentially nurturing places of resistance, real-and-imagined, material-and-metaphorical meeting grounds for struggle over all forms of oppression...'. While the *'third space'* within cultural studies is conceptualized as a 'place' where identity is negotiated and redefined, power structures are resisted, and life in its complexity, ambiguity and hybridity is performed, Soja (1996) seeks to locate his concept of 'thirdspace' in terms of the real and imagined. Here he draws also on the work of Lefebrve (1991), who suggested that it was possible to identify three different but co-existing spaces: the 'perceived' space of (material) spatial practice; the 'conceived' space, that is the representation of space; and the 'lived' space of representation – usually understood in terms of the merging of the 'perceived' and the 'conceived'. Building on this framework, Soja seeks to suggest that thirdspace is a particular type of spatial consciousness that goes beyond the mixing of the real and the imagined. Thirdspace exists in relationship/dialogue with first and second space as a:

> spatial awareness ... a product of a 'thirding' of the spatial imagination, by the creation of another mode of thinking about space that draws upon the material and mental spaces of the traditional dualism but extends well beyond them in scope, substance, and meaning. (Soja, 1996: 11)

The concept of the thirdspace is thus capable of incorporating and extending a range of related notions, to wit, following Moles (2008: n.p.), it is possible to say that:

> Thirdspace must be understood as an 'open-ended set of defining moments' (Soja, 1996: 260), a concept that speaks to various different theoretical ideas and draws them into its wide understanding. As such, we should understand Lefebvre's lived spaces (1991), Foucault's hetertopias [sic] (1986), bell hooks's [1990] homeplaces and Bhabha's (1991) thirdspace as part of the Thirdspace...

It is possible to conceptualize tourist space (physical, virtual and interacting) within the framework of the thirdspace. The thirdspace is where travellers, through their encounters with difference and the margins, are able to explore their identities as engaged and 'free' travellers. Tourism spaces are 'continually evolving landscapes with space for resistance, contestations, disruption and transgression of dominant discourses and wider hegemonic social and cultural relations' (Aitchison et al., 2000: 1). The tourist is a traveller who is capable of developing self–other experiences and relations that move beyond those that traditionally occur in the tourist space. It is here that a deeper understanding of place as cultural can play an important role. Objectified and imagined place is juxtaposed with 'being in place' in ways that make it possible to resist hegemonic, totalizing and disempowering constructions of the traveller and the travel Others. Commodified images and their discursive constructions can be disrupted and disassociated so that the re-inscription of place with an alternative sense of self and identity can be moved forward by the tourist.

Given the number of intersecting mobile elements, in particular the social interactions and inscribed meanings, that make up space and place, a variety of discourses may intersect in any one geographic location so that no one discourse has an absolute authority or legitimacy. Foucault refers to these contested places as heterotopias, 'the juxtaposing in a single real place, several spaces, several sites that are in themselves incompatible' (Foucault, 1986: 25). Edensor (1998 and 2000, cited in Ponting et al., 2005: 143) describes a continuum between 'heterogeneous' tourist spaces (likened to Foucault's heterotopias), in which tourism represents but one of many understandings of place, and 'enclavic' tourist spaces, those that are tightly controlled by the tourism industry. Edensor suggests that tourist space moves along this continuum as it becomes increasingly commodified by the tourism industry. What is most interesting, therefore, is to take these analyses and insights beyond the realm of resistance and the physical to a consideration of a tourism thirdspace that is constituted simultaneously through the interplay of the real-and-imagined.

Conclusion

Conceptualizing tourism through the lens of the thirdspace is to imagine it as a place imbued with the meanings, interpretations and stories of the various social actors who inhabit and pass through it. The contemporary travel space is one that is created as much by images, representations and global forms of communication technologies as it is by the physical. It is about commodification and resistance, signs and symbols. The experience can be the destination just as surely as it can be associated with arrival in place. And the journey/experience may be one which can occur through virtual reality and technologies such as IMAX. The notion of being there (home and away) is thus disrupted. Space, as it has been variously theorized here, has been shown to be inextricably linked with social interaction, discourse and power/knowledge relations. It is thus necessary to reconceptualize the spaces of tourism not as being either real or imagined, but as simultaneously real and imagined. This is the tourist thirdspace.

The notion of the thirdspace creates a fruitful framework for moving beyond the dichotomies of host/guest, traveller/tourist, self/Other and, significantly, *flâneur/choraster*, to an approach to understanding tourism and the travel experience that is interconnected and holistic. It may be, therefore, that the *choraster* is not a person or an assumed traveller identity that exists in isolation. It is not the insular traveller self. Nor is it a collective experience. The travel experience comes to be conceptualized as existing in a thirdspace, within which the traveller self is constituted and revealed. The thirdspace of travel is the place of both the real and the imaginary traveller and the real and imaginary travel experience – the 'imagined real' as Soja would argue. It is sensory and thus embraces the *flâneur* and the *choraster* (the visual and the experiential), but it cannot be reduced to either. The traveller as *choraster* thus does not exist in opposition to the traveller as *flâneur*. Rather, in the thirdspace they exist simultaneously, with each one containing the other.

8

Conclusion

The traveller self is formed and performed in the spaces and encounters of the travel experience. These selves, spaces and experiences comprise the tourist cultures that form the concerns of this book. They are simultaneously physical and mediated, real and imagined. They are comprised of images and stories as well as being negotiated in the context of meaningful engagements, and the serendipity and predictability of practice. At the centre of this contradictory landscape are the people, places and cultures of travel and the traveller. Since the Second World War, tourism has emerged to be one of the most significant pivots of the economies and cultures of cities and nations around the world. Contemporary tourism is a major source of employment and can be a motor for environmental, social and cultural change. Technological innovation, in particular that associated with aeronautical engineering, has been a major factor driving this increase in tourism. It is not that travel – both international and domestic – is new. It patently is not. What is new is the scale of contemporary tourism, including the relative accessibility of destinations, and the ease (and massification) of the travel experience. For some, these are markers of the democratization of travel and reasons to be optimistic about the consequences and possibilities of globalization. For others, however, they are evidence of the cultural and economic hegemony of the powerful 'developed' West/North over the 'developing' 'rest' – a harbinger of the destruction of local cultures and environments. Rather than pointing to objective truths and the reality of tourism, however, these positions point to the contradictions that define (and construct) the activity. Such contradictions have also prompted the development of a range of explanatory frames and different ways of seeing and understanding contemporary tourism. The negotiation of these perspectives in order to move beyond them has formed a central concern of this book.

With the emergence of mass tourism and the associated growth of the travel industry came the development of theories and perspectives from a range of academic disciplines. Some perspectives focused on the micro level of motivation and the individual looking to understand the reasons why people travel and the psychological factors driving them to seek out particular experiences and products. Other explanatory frameworks were concerned with looking more broadly at the social and economic forces and factors that were constructing and influencing travel and the tourism industry. Structures of power (and its imbalances) are important aspects of many such analyses. What came to be known as 'tourism platforms' were influential in framing the way in which tourism was studied from within broadly social scientific disciplines, such as sociology. Through the lens of the platform, tourism variously was regarded as being either positive for both the traveller and the destination or as having negative social and environmental 'impacts'. These impacts were always seen as objective and measurable – and hence potentially controllable. In acknowledging the negative dimensions of tourism, many commentators sought to find alternative platforms or approaches that were adaptive rather than formulaic. From these polarizing and mediating platforms emerged approaches that were concerned with the knowledges of tourism – with understanding tourism in terms of such concerns as conflict, interaction, play and strangerhood. Perhaps the most influential of the knowledge-based platforms, though, have been the studies of tourism that focused on the authenticity or otherwise of travel destinations and encounters in the travel space.

In the sociology of tourism literature, explanations of tourism couched in terms of seeking and experiencing authenticity dominate, with the work of Dean MacCannell being seminal. For MacCannell (1973, 1976), the contemporary tourist is something of a pilgrim who travels in order to experience and witness the authenticity of the places and cultures of the visited Other. Informed by his work, explanations of authenticity have tended to focus on the travel experience and on places and cultures as authentic. These forms or elements of authenticity, of course, are interconnected because the quality of the experience is very much understood as being determined by the authenticity of the encounter with the toured – in other words, encounters with 'real' places and the markers of 'real' cultures confirm a travel experience as being, or having been, authentic and thus meaningful. Frequently, though, as MacCannell points out, rather than having encounters with the authentic and the 'real', the tourist engages with or witnesses what MacCannell terms 'staged authenticity'. Staged authenticity refers to the artefacts, ceremonies and products which are performed and packaged, either by locals or the tourism industry, to stand in for the 'real' for the consumption of the visitor.

Many have built on the work of MacCannell in seeking to conceptualize the nature of the travel experience and to highlight its nuances, unpredictability and non-linearity. Wang (1999, 2000), for instance, is concerned to suggest that there are three dimensions to authenticity within travel – objective, constructed and existential. Here the emphasis shifts subtly but significantly away from measurable assessments of the reality or otherwise of the products and packages consumed by the tourist, to focus instead on the traveller self and the nature and interpretation of an individual's travel experiences. An engagement with the staged and the symbols of the 'real' can be as meaningful as encounters with the 'back stage'. Wang goes further, however, to highlight the importance of travel to the formation of the self. Similarly, John Urry's (2002) influential work on the tourist gaze pointed to the centrality of the sensory, in particular sight, to travel and tourist experiences. Urry also drew attention to the contrived and the simulated dimensions of tourism, suggesting that travel is often as much about the consumption of signs/sights as it is about encounters with authenticity and the 'real'. Significantly, Urry made reference to the evocative figure of the *flâneur* – a nineteenth-century literary construction who inhabited the arcades of Paris, consuming its spaces through the acts of looking and walking but never engaging.

Urry's work on the tourist gaze, and particularly his invocation of the idea of the *flâneur*, has underpinned the concerns of *Tourist Cultures*. The book set out to consider a number of intersecting themes in the study of tourism, including the relationship between tourism and identity, the significance of experience and memory to the construction of the traveller self, and the value of recent insights from sociology, geography and urban studies, in particular, to informing understandings of travel through a framework that places engagement and conceptions of the traveller space at its centre. Thus the idea of the *flâneur* was the starting point for developing a framework that situated travel and tourist cultures within the context of experience and place. In this respect, we follow Wearing and Wearing (1996) in suggesting that the notion of the *choraster* is useful in providing the conceptual space for imagining the traveller as being fully engaged with, and in, the travel experience and traveller space.

Travel is both the experience of immersion as well as of superficiality (and indeed, can involve the immersion in superficiality). The objective of *Tourist Cultures* was not to create a new way of understanding travel and tourism experiences, but to contribute to a significant body of work that exists within tourism studies and the sociology of tourism. A key guiding assumption in the book, therefore, is that a one-dimensional approach to the study of tourism is unsatisfying and unsatisfactory. It is nevertheless important to recognize the contributions that macro approaches make. Insights from studies of power, globalization and tourism, for instance, make it possible to appreciate that travel relationships are unequal and potentially damaging to local (host) cultures and environments and ways of life. The recognition of such effects points to a need to understand how these global trends and forces are actually experienced and engaged with 'on the ground', not only by local communities but also at the interface between the local and the traveller. The book sought to contribute to a way of understanding this intersection.

In seeking to explain tourism as a social practice, many of the most influential early works focused variously either on developing typologies of tourist activity and motivation or on examining the contribution which travel/tourism had made to the functioning of (Western) society and the maintenance of social structures. Tourism was frequently regarded as a good thing, which was also seen as bringing economic benefits to host destinations and thus as being something to be promoted. At the same time, however, influential contributions from Marxist scholars highlighted the exploitative nature of much travel and of the tourism industry. Marxists were concerned, in particular, with the commodification of destinations and the exploitation of local labour for the pursuit of profit. Tourism as a subset of leisure was regarded by Marxists as something of a commodified distraction. It was time away from paid (meaningful) work (see Chapter 3). Other commentators, however, wished to move beyond such narrow conceptualizations of tourism as being either good or bad, to focus instead on identifying and understanding different types of travellers and travel experiences. As was explored in Chapter 2, the work of Erik Cohen remains pivotal in highlighting both the differences in traveller type and their relationship to social institutions. Cohen, and those who followed him, moved the analysis of tourism away from examining its social function, to a concern instead with the traveller, highlighting that it was important to understand why people travelled – was it for mere pleasure, for instance, or were they engaged in a quest for meaningful experiences of other cultures?

Travel and tourism could no longer be regarded as homogeneous or monolithic. Rather, the theoretical groundwork was in place for interrogating the diversity, contradictions and complexities of travel and tourism activities and experiences. And what quickly became clear was that the most fruitful and incisive studies of tourism were those that considered it at both the macro levels of process and structure and the micro sites of the lived and the experiential. When the lived experiences of the traveller are considered in the context of broader concerns, such as power and exploitation, far richer and more nuanced understandings of the phenomenon are possible. Tourism is at once exploitative, destructive, rewarding and life-changing. It benefits local communities at the same time as it can erode or at least change local lifestyles and cultural practices. Our aim in this book was to work in the contours of these contradictions. Not to argue in favour of travel and tourism, but to engage with its indeterminacy.

Although situating tourism at the intersection of the macro and the micro, *Tourist Cultures* nevertheless focused in particular on the experiential and the lived dimensions of tourism and travel. It did this because it sought to understand tourism and travel as a space or a moment that is located outside established dichotomies. Thus we considered the different ways in which the search for 'authenticity' in travel has been understood both as an experience of the self and as a process whereby meaning and interpretative frames are negotiated and constructed. Tourists are not passive consumers of either destinations or their interpretation, but are instead actively engaged in a multi-sensory, embodied experience. While this experience may be individual, it is also cultural and occurs within, and with reference to, the tourist's own culture and meaning systems. What becomes necessary, then, is to find a way of understanding this intersection of culture and the self. Recent theorizing within sociology and cultural studies is particularly useful in that it highlights the need to understand that identities are shifting and decentred rather than fixed or given. It is now recognized that identity is no longer solely (or even principally) formed through the paid workforce, in the case of men, or the role of mother in the case of women. Rather, identity is understood as being fluid (liquid – as Bauman puts its). While key social categories of race, gender, class and ethnicity continue to be important, so too are cultural practices such as work, leisure and, significantly, travel.

In exploring the formation of traveller identity – or the traveller self, as we came to call it – the book considered key contributions by theorists from a range of disciplines, including the seminal work of psychologist Erik Erikson, which drew attention to identity formation as a process and the importance of autobiography or life story to this progression. Similarly, the social psychology of Herbert Mead has informed micro perspectives on the relationship between identity and society, including the work of influential sociologists, such as Anthony Giddens. For Giddens, self-identity formation is a reflexive project which occurs in the context of the increasing complexity of society and the shifting relationships between time and space. Individuals are positioned as being at the centre of their lives and their life narratives. We argue from a discussion of this work, and with reference to recent developments within tourism studies, that traveller narratives are central to the construction of the traveller self. Tourist consumption and the narration of a traveller identity, involve the reworking of the self through the incorporation of travel experiences and the places of travel. This process is one of ordering and filtering, of remembering and forgetting. It is about interpretation and encounters. Thus the images of travel and the products of the tourism industry are reworked continually through the travel experience and traveller encounters with the places and spaces of tourism. Indeed, the encounters of travel are central elements to the formation of the traveller self.

It is well documented within tourism studies that 'host–guest' relationships are often exploitative, particularly when the 'hosts' are from the developing 'South' and the 'guests' are from the affluent 'North'. But at the micro level these relationships can be harder to read. In Chapter 4, we examined some of the contradictory dimensions of the host–guest dichotomy, not to argue against macro analyses which highlight power differentials, but to try to understand the interactions and contingencies that inform the imagining of the traveller self and the travel experience. Tourism can provide a space for cross-cultural exchange and understanding. It can be an experiential framework for resisting cultural constraints and facilitating the crossing of cultural boundaries. Clearly, this is an idealistic position but it is one that should not be discounted. Seeking to find a language for expressing the potential of travel for promoting cultural understanding and engagement is important. Our task, however, has not been to provide this language, but simply to contribute in a small way to its formation.

The discussion of hosts and guests problematized a number of central conceptual dualisms that continue to be influential within tourism studies – host/guest, self/Other, traveller/tourist being noteworthy. But the discussion also pointed to the need to move any discussion of the traveller self beyond a concern with experience and embodiment alone to appreciate the centrality of the spaces and places of travel and tourism to the development of the traveller identity. Discussing the significance of space is not simply to refer to the physical landscape of travel – the 'real'. On the contrary, it is also to engage with and discuss the imaginary and symbolic spaces which frame the travel experience as well as increasingly come, if not to stand in for (replace) the physicality of travel, then to augment and (re)define its parameters. The second part of the book was devoted to a consideration of these issues and relationships. The spaces of travel were examined in terms of the real and the imaginary – another dichotomy that we subsequently sought to transcend. The real spaces of travel are the destinations – the beaches, the wildernesses and the cities, as well as the roads and transport links. Travel is about movement though space to place. It is about an engagement with visited and traversed places as well as with those encountered in the destination space. The travel circuit is one of movement and performance – departure, mobility, arrival, departure, mobility and arrival. Flows and located pauses, if you like. Also important are the artefacts and physical objects that surround the travelling/traveller body and that are encountered in the travel space. But the travel space is also about the metaphoric and the imaginative.

In seeking first to examine the intersection between travel and the tangible dimensions of space, in Chapter 5 two key tourism landscapes or destinations – the natural environment and the city – were discussed. Many have argued for the unity of the self and the environment and that travelling to natural areas can be explained in part in terms of a seeking out of a lost part of the self. While not wanting to advocate such a position, we do suggest, following the work of Wearing and Neil (1999), that it is timely for tourism studies to acknowledge that travel to natural environments can be a valuing of the landscape on its own terms, as well as an enhancement of the traveller self. Ecotourism approaches are wary of the commodification of nature by the tourism industry and argue instead for shifting the terms of the engagement away from the landscape as product and to privilege instead the experiences of the eco-traveller and his/her (spiritual and psychological) connections with nature and the landscape. While explorations of the importance of nature and travel seem to move quickly to positive (idealistic) considerations of its effects on the selves of travel, discussions of the traveller and the urban landscape are rarely couched in such positive, self-enhancing terms.

Cities are traditionally regarded as the antithesis of nature. The contrast between the rural and the urban – where the rural is the good and the safe, and the urban the dangerous and the bad – continues to permeate the urban studies literature (Stevenson, 2003). Understandings of urban tourism and its connection to the traveller self are similarly framed, at least implicitly, in terms of this dichotomy. The city is a place of excitement and contradictions, but it is also superficial and 'unnatural'. It contains spaces that are detached from the lived places of everyday life. Airports were discussed in this context and so too were those contrived tourist precincts that provide simulations and approximations of a city and its histories. As was suggested in Chapter 5, the *flâneur* was the original tourist of the urban and this perhaps remains the best metaphor by which to describe the ways in which many people experience cities as visitors – as spectators and voyeurs. A sense of place and the local is frequently replaced by seriality and anonymity. In attempting to access the 'back stages' of the urban tourist landscape, some travellers seek out the hidden spaces of suburbia, but in so doing they must write their own interpretative frames and ways of being a traveller in non-tourist urban space.

The spaces of travel are cultural and imaginary as well as physical and real. Ways of understanding the construction of travel and traveller identity in the context of the interplay between the globalization of travel and tourism and the cultural spaces of the local were canvassed in Chapter 6. In particular, it was suggested that a process of social valuing is a way of communicating the local to the visitor, of translating and transferring cultural meaning and local values. We suggested that most interesting in this context are the activities and priorities of young backpackers, who often seek out travel experiences in places outside the usual tourism itineraries in search of a space within which to engage with the cultures and places of the Other. And it is here that the predictability and serendipity of travel, mentioned above, become important. These experiences are both physical and emotional – the act of travelling becomes itself a space for the exploration of identity. Long-term independent travels have been described as secular rites of passage that involve immersion in the spaces of the local. Increasingly, though, the travel experiences of backpackers are as much about connections with home as they are about the experience of the spaces of away. Away comes to be constructed through an active dialogue with home as new technologies disrupt yet another taken-for-granted dualism of travel and pivot of the construction of the traveller self.

Communication technologies, such as the internet and mobile phones, mean that travellers can not only maintain regular contact with those outside the travel space, but can also use technology to narrate and receive feedback on their travel experiences and inter-pretations. The narrative that was once constructed through the writing of a personal journal over the course of a journey is for many now framed in the immediacy of the virtual. Images, too, which are central to the construction of the traveller self and the destination place, can be shared instantly with those at home, not as part of an over-arching reflection on the journey or as memory prompts for the forming of a traveller narrative, but as interactive commentaries on the 'now' of the travel moment. For some commentators, new technologies are contributing to the framing of the contemporary traveller as 'post-tourist'. For others, they are the latest influence in the negotiation of travel and the experiences of place, space and identity that frame and define it. What is clear, however, is that the old analytical frameworks are no longer adequate for explaining contemporary travel and the cultures of tourism. In particular, it is necessary to move away from the dichotomies or dualisms that are a feature of the discourse – home/away, tourist/traveller, self/Other, host/guest, being there/getting there, real/imaginary, to name but a few.

The work of Ed Soja (1996) and his idea of the thirdspace is useful here. Thirdspace is the imagined-real, a particular type of spatial consciousness that transcends existing dualisms while existing in dialogue with them. For understandings of travel, it makes it possible to develop an approach that is sensory and engaged, interconnected and holistic. The *choraster* or traveller self is thus not a fixed identity but a metaphor for the imagined-real spaces and experiences of travel that are contingent and shifting, meaningful and lived – circuits of engagement and dialogue. It is in accepting the challenge of imagining travel, and the traveller in terms of their contradictions and inconsistencies, that it becomes possible to start to understand the lived complexity of contemporary tourist cultures. The task of *Tourist*

Cultures was thus a simple and yet potentially important one. In drawing together ways of seeing and understanding travel in terms of its spaces and selves, the book contributed insights into what is one of the most significant of contemporary processes. It is in the imagined-real spaces of the traveller self that it may become possible to envisage tourist cultures and futures that will empower and engage.

References

Acland, C. (1998) 'Imaxtechnology and the tourist gaze', *Cultural Studies*, 12(3): 429–45.

Adler, J. (1985) 'Youth on the road: Reflections on the history of tramping', *Annals of Tourism Research*, 12(3): 335–54.

Aitchison, C. (1999) 'New cultural geographies: The spatiality of leisure, gender and sexuality', *Leisure Studies*, 18(1): 19–40.

Aitchison, C. (2001) 'Theorizing other discourses of tourism, gender and culture: Can the subaltern speak (in tourism)?', *Tourist Studies*, 1(2): 133–47.

Aitchison, C. (2005) 'Feminist and gender perspectives in tourism studies: The social-cultural nexus of critical and cultural theories', *Tourist Studies*, 5(3): 207–24.

Aitchison, C., MacLeod, N.E. and Shaw, S.J. (2000) *Leisure and Tourism Landscapes: Social and Cultural Geographies*. London: Routledge.

Aitchison, C. and Reeves, C. (1998) 'Gendered (bed)spaces: The culture and commerce of women only tourism', in C. Aitchison and F. Jordan (eds), *Gender, Space and Identity: Leisure, Culture and Commerce*. Eastbourne: Leisure Studies Association. pp. 47–68.

Aldridge, A. (2003) *Consumption*. Cambridge: Polity Press.

Allen, L.R. (1991) 'Benefits of leisure services to community satisfaction', in B.L. Driver, P.J. Brown and G.L. Peterson (eds), *Benefits of Leisure*. State College, PA: Venture. pp. 331–50.

Amin, A. and Thrift, N. (2002) *Cities: Reimagining the Urban*. Cambridge: Polity Press.

Aramberri, J. (2001) 'The host should get lost: Paradigms in the tourism theory', *Annals of Tourism Research*, 28(3): 738–61.

Arellano, A. (2004) 'Bodies, spirits, and Incas: Performing Machu Picchu', in M. Sheller and J. Urry (eds), *Tourism Mobilities: Places to Play, Places in Play*. London and New York: Routledge. pp. 67–77.

Atkinson, P. and Housley, W. (2003) *Interactionism*. London: SAGE.

Australian Heritage Commission (1992) *What is Social Value? A Discussion Chapter*. Technical Publications Series Number 3. Canberra: AGPS.

Bammell, G. and Bammell, L. (1992) *Leisure and Human Behavior*. Dubuque, IA: W.C. Brown.

Barthes, R. (1973) *Mythologies*. Trans. A. Lavers. London: Paladin.

Bauman, Z. (2000) *Liquid Modernity*. Cambridge: Polity Press.

Bauman, Z. (2001) *The Individualized Society*. Cambridge: Polity Press.

Benjamin, W. (1973) *Charles Baudelaire: A Lyric Poet in the Era of High Capitalism*. Trans. H. Zohn. London: New Left Books.

Bennett, T. (1998) *Culture: A Reformer's Science*. Sydney: Allen & Unwin.

Bhabha, H. (1990) 'The third space: Interview with Homi K. Bhabha', in J. Rutherford (ed.), *Identity: Community, Culture, Difference*. London: Lawrence & Wishart. pp. 207–21.

Bhabha, H. (1991) 'Caliban speaks to Prospero: Cultural identity and the crisis of representation', in P. Marini (ed.), *Critical Fictions: The Politics of Imaginative Writing*. Seattle: Bay Press. pp. 62–5.

Bhabha, H. (1994) *The Location of Culture*. London: Routledge.

Bhattacharya, K. (2006) 'Non-western traditions: Leisure in India', in C. Rojek, S.M. Shaw and A.J. Veal (eds), *A Handbook of Leisure Studies*. Basingstoke: Palgrave Macmillan. pp. 75–91.

Bookchin, M. (1982) *The Ecology of Freedom: The Emergence and Dissolution of Hierarchy*. Palo Alto, CA: Palo Alto Publishing.

Boorstin, D. (1987) *The Image: A Guide to Pseudo-events in America* (25th Anniversary Edition). New York: Atheneum.

Böröcz, J. (1996) *Leisure Migration: A Sociological Study*. Oxford: Pergamon Press.

Bourdieu, P. (1984) *Distinction: A Social Critique of Judgement and Taste*. Cambridge, MA: Harvard University Press.

Brammer, N., Beech, J. and Burns, P. (2004) 'Use and abuse of tourism: The Goan experience', *Tourism Culture & Communication*, 5(1): 23–35.

Brennan, A. (1996) 'Ethics, ecology and economics', in N.S. Cooper and R.C.J. Carling (eds), *Ecologists and Ethical Judgements*. London: Chapman & Hall Ltd. pp. 13–26.

Britton, S. (1991) 'Tourism, capital and place: Towards a critical geography of tourism', *Environment and Planning D: Society and Space*, 9(4): 451–78.

Britton, S. (1996) 'Tourism, dependency, and development: A mode of analysis', in Y. Apostolopoulos, S. Leivadi and A. Yiannakis (eds), *The Sociology of Tourism*. London: Routledge. pp. 155–72.

Brohman, J. (1996) 'New directions in tourism for Third World development', *Annals of Tourism Research*, 23(1): 48–70.

Brown, G. (1992) 'Tourism and symbolic consumption', in P. Johnson and B. Thomas (eds), *Choice and Demand in Tourism*. London: Mansel. pp. 57–71.

Brown, P.R., Brown, W.J. and Powers, J.R. (2001) 'Time pressure, satisfaction with leisure and health among Australian women', *Annals of Leisure Research*, 4: 1–16.

Bruner, E.M. (1991) 'Transformation of self in tourism', *Annals of Tourism Research*, 18: 238–50.

Buhalis, D. (2001) 'The tourism phenomenon: The new tourist and consumer', in S. Wahan and C. Cooper (eds), *Tourism in the Age of Globalisation*. London: Routledge. pp. 69–96.

Butcher, J. (1997) 'Sustainable development or development?', in M.J. Stabler (ed.), *Tourism and Sustainability: Principles to Practice*. Wallingford: CAB International. pp. 27–38.

Butcher, J. (2000) 'The "new tourist" as anthropologist', in M. Robinson, P. Long, N. Evans, R. Sharpley and J. Swarbrooke (eds), *Reflections on International Tourism: Motivations, Behaviour and Tourist Types*. Sunderland: Centre for Travel and Tourism in Association with Business Education Publishers. pp. 45–54.

Butcher, J. (2003) *The Moralisation of Tourism: Sun, Sand ... and Saving the World?* London: Routledge.

Castells, M. (2004) *The Information Age: Economy, Society and Culture*. Vol. 2, *The Power of Identity* (2nd edn). Malden, MA: Blackwell.

Ceballos-Lascurain, H. (1992) 'Tourism, ecotourism, and protected areas: The state of nature-based tourism around the world and guidelines for its development', paper presented at the IVth World Congress on National Parks and Protected Areas, Caracas, Venezuela.

Chambers, E. (1997) 'Introduction: Tourism's mediators', in E. Chambers (ed.), *Tourism and Culture: An Applied Perspective*. Albany, NY: State University of New York Press. pp. 1–11.

Chan, Y.W. (2006) 'Coming of age of the Chinese tourists: The emergence of non-Western tourism and host–guest interactions in Vietnam's border tourism', *Tourist Studies*, 6(3): 187–213.

Cheong, S. and Miller, M. (2000) 'Power and tourism: A Foucauldian observation', *Annals of Tourism Research*, 27(2): 371–90.

Cixous, H. (1983) 'The laugh of the Medusa', in E. Abel and E.K. Abel (eds), *The Signs Reader: Women, Gender, and Scholarship*. Chicago: University of Chicago Press. pp. 279–97.

Clarke, J., Hall, S., Jefferson, T. and Roberts, B. (1975) 'Subcultures, cultures and class: A theoretical overview', in S. Hall and T. Jefferson (eds), *Resistance through Rituals Youth Subcultures in Post-War Britain*. London: Hutchinson. pp. 9–74.

Clifford, J. (1992) 'Travelling cultures', in L. Grossberg, C. Nelson and P. Treichler (eds), *Cultural Studies*. London: Routledge. pp. 96–111.

Clifford, J. (1997) *Routes: Travel and Translation in the Late Twentieth Century*. Cambridge, MA: Harvard University Press.

Cloke, P. and Perkins, H.C. (1998) '"Cracking the canyon with the awesome foursome": Presentations of adventure tourism in New Zealand', *Environment and Planning D: Society and Space*, 16(3): 185–218.

Cockburn-Wootten, C., Friend, L. and McIntosh, A. (2006) 'A discourse analysis of representational spaces: Writings of women independent traveller', *Tourism*, 54(1): 7–16.

Cohen, E. (1972) 'Towards a sociology of international tourism', *Social Research*, 39(1): 164–82.

Cohen, E. (1973) 'Nomads from affluence: Notes on the phenomenon of drifter tourism', *International Journal of Comparative Sociology*, XIV (1–2): 89–103.

Cohen, E. (1974) 'Who is a tourist? A conceptual classification', *The Sociological Review*, 22(4): 527–55.

Cohen, E. (1979) 'A phenomenology of tourist experiences', *Sociology*, 13: 179–201.

Cohen, E. (1984) 'The sociology of tourism: Approaches, issues and findings', *Annual Review of Sociology*, 10: 373–92.

Cohen, E. (1987) 'Alternative tourism: A critique', *Tourism Recreation Research*, 12(2): 13–18.

Cohen, E. (1988) 'Authenticity and commoditization in tourism', *Annals of Tourism Research*, 15: 371–86.

Cohen, E. (2001) 'Ethnic tourism in Southeast Asia', in C.-B. Tan, C.-H. Sidney, Y.-H. Cheung (eds), *Tourism, Anthropology and China*. Singapore: White Lotus Press. pp. 27–53.

Cohen, E. (2004) *Contemporary Tourism: Diversity and Change*. Oxford: Elsevier.

Cohen, P. (1968) *Modern Social Theory*. New York: Basic Books.

Cohen, S. and Taylor, L. (1976) *Escape Attempts*. Harmondsworth: Penguin.

Cole, S. (2006) 'Cultural tourism, community participation and empowerment', in M.K. Smith and M. Robinson (eds), *Cultural Tourism in a Changing World: Politics, Participation and (Re)presentation*. Bristol: Channel View Publications. pp. 89–103.

Cole, S. (2007) 'Beyond authenticity and commodification', *Annals of Tourism Research*, 34(4): 943–60.

Craik, J. (1991) *Resorting to Tourism: Cultural Policies for Tourist Development in Australia*. North Sydney: Allen & Unwin.

Craik, J. (1997) 'The culture of tourism', in C. Rojek and J. Urry (eds), *Touring Cultures: Transformations of Travel and Theory*. London: Routledge. pp. 113–36.

Craik, J. (1998) 'Interpretative mismatch in cultural tourism', *Tourism, Culture and Communication*, 1(1): 115–28.

Craik, J. (2001) 'Tourism, culture and national identity', in T. Bennett and D. Carter (eds), *Culture in Australia: Policies, Publics and Programs*. Cambridge: Cambridge University Press. pp. 89–113.

Crang, M. (1997) 'Picturing practices: Research through the tourist gaze', *Progress in Human Geography*, 21(3): 359–73.

Crawshaw, C. and Urry, J. (1997) 'Tourism and the photographic eye', in C. Rojek and J. Urry (eds), *Touring Cultures: Transformations of Travel and Theory*. London and New York: Routledge. pp. 176–95.

Crick, M. (1989) 'Representations of international tourism in the social sciences: Sun, sex, sights, savings, and servility', *Annual Review of Anthropology*, 18: 307–44.

Critcher, C. (2006) 'A touch of class', in C. Rojek, S.M. Shaw and A.J. Veal (eds), *A Handbook of Leisure Studies*. London: Palgrave Macmillan. pp. 271–87.

Crompton, J.L. (1979) 'Motivations for pleasure vacation', *Annals of Tourism Research*, 6(4): 408–24.

Cross, G. (1993) *Time and Money: The Making of Consumer Culture*. London: Routledge.

Crouch, D. (1999) 'Introduction: Encounters in leisure/tourism', in D. Crouch (ed.), *Leisure/Tourism Geographies: Practices and Geographical Knowledge*. London: Routledge. pp. 1–16.

Crouch, D. (2000) 'Places around us: Embodied lay geographies in leisure and tourism', *Leisure Studies*, 19(2): 63–76.

Crouch, D. (2001) 'Spatialities and the feeling of doing', *Social and Cultural Geography*, 2(1): 61–75.

Crouch, D., Aronsson, L. and Wahlstrom, L. (2001) 'Tourist encounters', *Tourist Studies*, 1(3): 253–70.

Crouch, D. and Desforges, L. (2003) 'The sensuous in the tourist encounter: Introduction: The power of the body in tourist studies', *Tourist Studies*, 3(1): 5–22.

Csikszentmihalyi, M. (1990) *Flow: The Psychology of Optimal Experience*. New York: HarperCollins.

Culler, J. (1981) 'Semiotics of tourism', *American Journal of Semiotics*, 1: 172–40.

Cunningham, P. (2006) 'Social valuing for Ogasawara as a place and space among ethnic host', *Tourist Management*, 27(3): 505–16.

Curtis, B. and Pajaczkowska, C. (1994) 'Getting there: Travel, time and narrative', in G. Robertson, M. Mash, L. Tickner, J. Bird, B. Curtis and T. Putnam (eds), *Traveller's Tales: Narratives of Home and Displacement*. London: Routledge. pp. 199–215.

Dann, G. (1977) 'Anomie, ego-enhancement and tourism', *Annals of Tourism Research*, 4(4): 184–94.

Dann, G. (1993) 'Advertising in tourism and travel: Tourism brochures', in M. Khan, M. Olsen and T. Var (eds), *Encyclopaedia of Travel and Tourism*. New York: Van Nostrand Reinhold. pp. 893–901.

Dann, G. (1996) *The Language of Tourism: A Sociolinguistic Perspective*. Wallingford: CAB International.

Dann, G. (2000) 'Theoretical advances in the sociological treatment of tourism', in S. Quah and A. Sales (eds), *The International Handbook of Sociology*. London: SAGE. pp. 367–84.

Dann, G. and Jacobson, J. (2003) 'Tourism smellscapes', *Tourism Geographies*, 5(1): 3–25.

Darcy, S. (2007) *Accessible Tourism: A Universal and Global Perspective*. Wallingford: CAB International.

Deegan, M.J. (1998) 'Weaving the American ritual tapestry', in M.J. Deegan (ed.), *The American Ritual Tapestry: Social Rules and Cultural Meanings*. Westport, CT: Greenwood Press. pp. 3–17.

Deem, R. (1986) *All Work and No Play? The Sociology of Women and Leisure*. Milton Keynes: Open University Press.

de Albuquerque, K. (1998) 'Sex, beach boys and female tourists in the Caribbean', in B.M. Dank (ed.), *Sex Work and Sex Workers*. Vol. 2, *Sexuality and Culture*. New Brunswick, NJ: Transaction. pp. 87–111.

de Graff, J. (ed.) (2003) *Take Back Your Time: Fighting Overwork and Time Poverty in America*. San Francisco, CA: Berrett-Koehler.

de Grazia, S. (1964) *Of Time, Work and Leisure*. Garden City, NY: Anchor Books.

Desforges, L. (1998) 'Checking out the planet: Global representations, local identities and youth travel', in T. Skelton and G. Valentine (eds), *Cool*

Places: Geographies of Youth Cultures. London and New York: Routledge. pp. 175–92.

Desforges, L. (2000) 'Travelling the world: Identity and travel biography', *Annals of Tourism Research*, 27(4): 926–45.

Devall, B. (1988) *Simple in Means, Rich in Ends: Practicing Deep Ecology*. Layton, UT: Gibbs Smith Publisher.

Dickson, T.J., Laneyrie, F. and Pritchard, A. (2006) 'Australian snowsports: Gendered and contested spaces?', *Tourism*, 54(1): 17–32.

Donald, S. and Gammack, G. (2007) *Tourism and the Branded City: Film and Identity on the Pacific Rim*. Aldershot: Ashgate.

Doron, A. (2005) 'Encountering the 'Other': Pilgrims, tourists and boatmen in the city of Varanasi', *The Australian Journal of Anthropology*, 16(2): 157–78.

Drake, J.D. (2001) *Downshifting: How to Work Less and Enjoy Life More*. San Francisco, CA: Berrett-Koehler.

Driver, B.L., Brown, P.J. and Peterson, G.L. (eds) (1991) *Benefits of Leisure*. State College, PA: Venture.

Dumazedier, J. (1967) *Toward a Society of Leisure*. New York: Macmillan.

Eadington, W. and Smith, V. (1992) 'Introduction: The emergence of alternative forms of tourism', in V. Smith and W. Eadington (eds), *Tourism Alternatives: Potentials and Problems in the Development of Tourism*. Philadelphia: University of Pennsylvania Press. pp. 1–12.

Edensor, T. (1998) *Tourists at the Taj: Performance and Meaning at a Symbolic Site*. London and New York: Routledge.

Edensor, T. (2000) 'Staging tourism: Tourists as performers', *Annals of Tourism Research*, 27(2): 322–44.

Edensor, T. (2001) 'Performing tourism, staging tourism: (Re)producing tourist space and practice', *Tourist Studies*, 1(1): 59–81.

Edward, H., Garcia, R. and DeMoya, T. (2001) 'Female tourists and beach boys: Romance or sex tourism?', *Annals of Tourism Research*, 28(4): 978–97.

Elden, S. (2001) *Mapping the Present: Heidegger, Foucault and the Project of Spatial History*. New York: Continuum.

Eliade, M. (1960) *Myths, Dreams and Mysteries*. Trans. P. Mairet. London: Harvill Press.

Elsrud, T. (2001) 'Risk creation in traveling: Backpacker adventure narration', *Annals of Tourism Research*, 28(3): 597–617.

Erikson, E.H. (1963) *Childhood and Society* (2nd edn). New York: W.W. Norton.

Erikson, E.H. (1971) *Identity, Youth and Crisis*. London: Faber & Faber.

Erikson, E.H. (1975) *Life History and the Historical Moment*. New York: W.W. Norton.

Everingham, C. (2002) 'Engendering time: Gender, equity and discourses of workplace flexibility', *Time and Society*, 11(2–3): 335–51.

Farina, J. (1980) 'Perceptions of time', in T. Goodall and P. Witt (eds), *Recreation and Leisure: Issues in an Era of Change* (3rd edn). State College, PA: Venture. pp. 20–41.

Favero, P. (2007) '"What a wonderful world!": On the "touristic ways of seeing", the knowledge and the politics of the "culture industries of otherness"', *Tourist Studies*, 7(1): 51–81.

Feifer, M. (1986) *Tourism in History: From Imperial Rome to the Present*. New York: Stein & Day.

Fevre, R. (2003) *The New Sociology of Economic Behaviour*. Thousand Oaks, CA: SAGE.

Fly, J. (1986) 'Nature, outdoor recreation and tourism: The basis for regional population growth in northern lower Michigan', unpublished PhD dissertation, University of Michigan, Michigan.

Foucault, M. (1961) *Madness and Civilization: A History of Insanity in the Age of Reason*. Trans. R. Howard. London: Routledge.

Foucault, M. (1975) *Discipline and Punish: The Birth of the Prison*. Trans. A. Sheridan. London: Penguin.

Foucault, M. (1986) 'Of other spaces', *Diacritics*, 16(1): 22–7.

Franklin, A. (2003) 'The tourist syndrome: An interview with Zygmunt Bauman', *Tourist Studies*, 3(2): 205–17.

Franklin, A. and Crang, M. (2001) 'The trouble with tourism and travel theory?', *Tourist Studies*, 1(1): 5–22.

Frederick, C.J. and Shaw, S.M. (1995) 'Body image as a leisure constraint: Examining the experience of aerobic exercise classes for young women', *Leisure Sciences*, 17(2): 57–73.

Friedman, J. (1994) *Cultural Identity and Global Process*. London: SAGE.

Frisby, D. (1986) *Fragments of Modernity: Theories of Modernity in the Work of Simmel, Kracauer and Benjamin*. Cambridge, MA: MIT Press.

Frow, J. (1997) *Time and Commodity Culture: Essays in Cultural Theory and Postmodernity*. Oxford: Clarendon Press.

Fullagar, S. (2002) 'Narratives of travel: Desire and the movement of feminine subjectivity', *Leisure Studies*, 21: 57–74.

Gable, E. and Handler, R. (2000) 'Public history, private memory: Notes from the ethnography of Colonial Williamsburg, Virginia, USA', *Ethnos*, 65(2): 237–52.

Galani-Moutafi, V. (2000) 'The self and the other: Traveller, ethnographer, tourist', *Annals of Tourism Research*, 27(1): 203–24.

Game, A. (1991) *Undoing the Social: Towards a Deconstructive Sociology*. Milton Keynes: Open University Press.

Garton, A., Harvey, R. and Price, C. (2004) 'Influence of perceived family environment on adolescent leisure participation', *Australian Journal of Psychology*, 56(1): 18–24.

Gaskell, K. (2007) 'Virtual tourism takes off', *Perth Now*, 29 June. Retrieved 10 October 2008, from http://www.news.com.au/perthnow/story/0,21598, 21988439-5005040,00.html

Gergen, K. (1991) *The Saturated Self: Dilemmas of Identity in Contemporary Life*. New York: Basic Books.

Giddens, A. (1987) 'Structuralism, post-structuralism and the production of culture', in A. Giddens and J.H. Turner (eds), *Social Theory Today*. Cambridge: Polity Press. pp. 195–223.

Giddens, A. (1991) *Modernity and Self-identity: Self and Society in the Late Modern Age*. Stanford, CA: Stanford University Press.

Giddens, A. (2006) *Sociology* (5th edn). Cambridge: Polity Press.

Glasser, W. (1972) *The Identity Society*. New York: Harper & Row.

Godbey, G. and Robinson, J. (1997) 'The increasing prospects for leisure', *Parks and Recreation*, 32(6): 75–82.

Godfrey-Smith, W. (1980) 'The value of wilderness: A philosophical approach', in R.W. Robertson, P. Helman and A. Davey (eds), *Wilderness Management in Australia: Proceedings of a Symposium at the Canberra College of Advanced Education 19–23 July*. Canberra: Canberra College of Advanced Education. pp. 56–71.

Graburn, N. (1983) 'The anthropology of tourism', *Annals of Tourism Research*, 10(1): 9–33.

Graburn, N.H.H. (1989) 'Tourism: The sacred journey', in V.L. Smith (ed.), *Hosts and Guests: The Anthropology of Tourism*. Philadelphia: University of Pennsylvania Press. pp. 21–36.

Gramsci, A. (1971) *Selections from the Prison Notebooks of Antonio Gramsci*. Trans. Q. Hoare and G. Nowell Smith. London: Lawrence & Wishart.

Grint, K. (2005) *The Sociology of Work* (3rd edn). Cambridge: Polity Press.

Grosz, E. (1986) 'Conclusion: What is feminist theory?', in C. Pateman and E. Grosz (eds), *Feminist Challenges*. Sydney: Allen & Unwin. pp. 190–204.

Grosz, E. (1995a) *Space, Time and Perversion: Essays on the Politics of Body*. London: Routledge.

Grosz, E. (1995b) 'Women, chora, dwelling', in S. Watson and K. Gibson (eds), *Postmodern Cities and Spaces*. Oxford: Blackwell. pp. 47–58.

Guignon, C. (1993) 'Authenticity, moral values, and psychotherapy', in C. Guignon (ed.), *The Cambridge Companion to Heidegger*. Cambridge: Cambridge University Press. pp. 215–39.

Guignon, C. (2002) 'Hermeneutics, authenticity, and the aims of psychology', *Journal of Theoretical and Philosophical Psychology*, 22(2): 83–102.

Guignon, C. (2004) *On Being Authentic*. London: Routledge.

Gustafson, P. (2001) 'Meanings of place: Everyday experience and theoretical conceptualizations', *Journal of Environmental Psychology*, 21(1): 5–16.

Halgreen, T. (2004) 'Tourist in the concrete desert', in M. Sheller and J. Urry (eds), *Tourism Mobilities: Places to Place, Places in Play*. London and New York: Routledge. pp. 143–54.

Hall, C.M. (1994) *Tourism and Politics: Power, Policy and Place*. Chichester: John Wiley & Sons.

Hall, C.M. (1996) 'Gender and economic interests in tourism prostitution: The nature, development and implications of sex tourism in South-East Asia', in Y. Apostolopoulos, S. Leivadi and A. Yiannakis (eds), *The Sociology of Tourism: Theoretical and Empirical Investigations*. London: Routledge. pp. 265–80.

Hall, C.M. (2000) *Tourism Policy: A Public Policy Approach*. Harlow: Pearson Education.

Hall, C.M. (2004) 'Reflexivity and tourism research: Situating myself and/with others', in J. Phillimore and L. Goodson (eds), *Qualitative Research in*

Tourism: Ontologies, Epistemologies and Methodologies. London: Routledge. pp. 137–55.

Hall, C.M. and McArthur, S. (1991) 'Commercial white water rafting in Australia', *Leisure Options*, 1(2): 15–21.

Hall, C.M. and Page, S. (1999) *The Geography of Tourism and Recreation: Environment, Place and Space* (2nd edn). London: Routledge.

Hall, C.M. and Tucker, H. (eds) (2004) *Tourism and Postcolonialism: Contested Discourses, Identities and Representations*. London: Routledge.

Hall, S. (1996) 'Introduction: Who needs identity?', in S. Hall and P. Du Gay (eds), *Questions of Cultural Identity*. London: SAGE. pp. 1–17.

Hamilton, C. (2003) *Growth Fetish*. Sydney: Allen & Unwin.

Hamilton, C. and Mail, E. (2003) 'Downshifting in Australia: A sea-change in the pursuit of happiness'. Discussion Paper No. 50. Canberra: The Australia Institute.

Hamilton-Smith, E. (1987) 'Four kinds of tourism?', *Annals of Tourism Research*, 14(3): 332–44.

Harrison, J. (2003) *Being a Tourist: Finding Meaning in Pleasure Travel*. Vancouver and Toronto: UBC Press.

Hay, R.B. (1988) 'Toward a theory of sense of place', *The Trumpeter*, 5: 159–64.

Haywood, K.M. (1988) 'Responsible and responsive tourism planning in the community', *Tourism Management*, 9(2): 105–18.

Hochschild, A. (1997) *The Time Bind: When Work Becomes Home and Home Becomes Work*. New York: Metropolitan Books.

Holden, A. (2000) *Environment and Tourism*. London and New York: Routledge.

Holland, A. (1996) 'The use and abuse of ecological concepts in environmental ethics', in N.S. Cooper and R.C.J. Carling (eds), *Ecologists and Ethical Judgements*. London: Chapman & Hall Ltd. pp. 27–42.

Hollinshead, K. (1998) 'Tourism, hybridity, and ambiguity: The relevance of Bhabha's "third space" cultures', *Journal of Leisure Research*, 30(1): 121–56.

Hollinshead, K. (2000) 'Bhabha and the fantasmatics of the restless, contemporary world: The translation of Bhabhian thought on hybridity and enunciation to the transdisciplinary realms of tourism studies', paper presented at The Travelling Concepts: Text, Subjectivity, Hybridity Conference, Amsterdam.

Hollinshead, K. (2004) 'Tourism and new sense: Worldmaking and the enunciative value of tourism', in C.M. Hall and H. Tucker (eds), *Tourism and Postcolonialism: Contested Discourses, Identities and Representations*. London: Routledge. pp. 25–42.

Hom Cary, S. (2004) 'The tourist moment', *Annals of Tourism Research*, 31(1): 61–77.

hooks, b. (1990) *Yearning: Race, Gender, and Cultural Politics*. Boston, MA: South End Press.

Hubbard, P., Kitchin, R. and Valentine, G. (eds) (2004) *Key Thinkers on Space and Place*. Thousand Oaks, CA: SAGE.

Hughes, G. (1995) 'Authenticity in tourism', *Annals of Tourism Research*, 22(4): 781–803.

Irigaray, L. (1986) 'The sex which is not one' (trans. C. Reeder), in E. Marks and I. de Courtivron (eds), *New French Feminisms*. Brighton: Harvester Press. pp. 99–106.

Irigaray, L. (2004) *An Ethics of Sexual Difference*. London: Continuum.

Iso-Ahola, S.E. (1980) *The Social Psychology of Leisure and Recreation*. Dubuque, IA: W.C. Brown.

Ittelsen, W.H., Proshansky, H.M. and Rivilin, L.G. (1974) *An Introduction to Environmental Psychology*. New York: Holt, Rinehart & Winston.

Jack, G. and Phipps, A.M. (2005) *Tourism and Intercultural Exchange: Why Tourism Matters*. Clevedon: Channel View Publications.

Jackson, E.L. (ed.) (2005) *Constraints to Leisure*. State College, PA: Venture.

Jafari, J. (1989) 'An English language literature review', in J. Bystrzanowski (ed.), *Tourism as a Factor of Change: A Sociocultural Study*. Vienna: Centre for Research and Documentation in the Social Sciences. pp. 17–60.

Jamieson, S. (1962) 'Regional factors in industrial conflict: The case of British Columbia', *Journal of Economics and Political Science*, 28: 405–16.

Jenkins, C. and Sherman, B. (1979) *The Collapse of Work*. London: Methuen.

Jenkins, O.H. (2000) Tourist destination images and stereotypes: A study of backpacker images of Australia', unpublished doctoral thesis, University of Queensland, Geographical Sciences and Planning.

Jenkins, O.H. (2003) 'Photography and travel brochures: The circle of representation', *Tourism Geographies*, 5(3): 305–28.

Jensen, J. (1998) *The Nashville Sound: Authenticity, Commercialisation and Country Music*. Nashville, TN: Country Music Foundation Press and Vanderbilt University Press.

Jiang, J., Havitz, M.E. and O'Brien, R.M. (2000) 'Validating the international tourist role scale', *Annals of Tourism Research*, 27(4): 964–81.

Johnson, P. (2006) 'Unpacking the bags: Cultural literacy and cosmopolitanism in women's travel writings about the Islamic Republic, 1979–2002', unpublished PhD dissertation, The University of Newcastle, Australia.

Jokinen, E. and Veijola, S. (1997) 'The disoriented tourist: The figuration of the tourist in contemporary cultural critique', in C. Rojek and J. Urry (eds), *Touring Cultures: Transformations of Travel and Theory*. London: Routledge. pp. 23–51.

Jordan, F. and Gibson, H. (2005) 'We're not stupid. But we'll not stay home either: Experiences of solo women travellers', *Tourism Review International*, 9(2): 195–211.

Kando, T.M. (1980) *Leisure and Popular Culture in Transition* (2nd edn). St Louis, MO: C.V. Mosby Company.

Kaplan, R. and Kaplan, S. (1989) *The Experience of Nature: A Psychological Perspective*. Cambridge: Cambridge University Press.

Kelly, I. (1997) 'Study tours: A model for "benign" tourism?', *Journal of Tourism Studies*, 8(1): 42–51.

Kelly, J. (1983) *Leisure Identities and Interactions*. London: Allen & Unwin.

Kelly, J. (1987) *Freedom to Be: A New Sociology of Leisure*. New York: Macmillan.

Kelly, J. (1994) 'The symbolic interaction metaphor and leisure: Critical challenges', *Leisure Studies*, 13: 81–96.

Kielbasiewicz-Drozdowska, I. (2005) 'Leisure time as a space for gaining social capital', *Studies in Physical Culture and Tourism*, 12(1): 73–7.

Kinnaird, V., Kothari, U. and Hall, D. (1994) 'Tourism: Gender perspectives', in V. Kinnaird and D. Hall (eds), *Tourism: A Gender Analysis*. Chichester: John Wiley & Sons. pp. 1–34.

Krippendorf, J. (1987) *The Holiday Makers*. London: Heinemann.

Larrabee, E. and Meyersohn, R. (1958) *Mass Leisure*. New York: Free Press.

Lash, S. and Urry, J. (1994) *Economies of Signs and Space*. London: SAGE.

Law, C. (1992) 'Urban tourism and its contribution to economic regeneration', *Urban Studies*, 29: 599–618.

Law, L. (1997) 'Dancing on the bar: Sex, money and the uneasy politics of the third space', in S. Pile and M. Keith (eds), *Geographies of Resistance*. London: Routledge. pp. 107–23.

Lechte, J. (1995) '(Not) belonging in postmodern space', in S. Watson and K. Gibson (eds), *Postmodern Cities and Spaces*. Oxford: Blackwell. pp. 97–111.

Lefebvre, H. (1976) *The Survival of Capitalism*. London: Allen & Unwin.

Lefebvre, H. (1991) *The Production of Space*. Oxford: Blackwell.

Leopold, A. (1949) *A Sand Country Almanac*. London: Oxford University Press.

Leung, P. (2002) 'Tourism and economic development of less developed countries: The case of Cambodia', *Tourism Recreation Research*, 27(1): 91–102.

Levenstein, H. (1998) *Seductive Journey: American Tourists in France from Jefferson to the Jazz Age*. Chicago: University of Chicago Press.

Lévi-Strauss, C. (1964) *Totemism*. London: Merlin Press.

Lew, A. (2003) 'Editorial: Tourism in places and places in tourism', *Tourism Geographies*, 5(3): 121–2.

Li, Y. (2000) 'Geographical consciousness and tourism experience', *Annals of Tourism Research*, 27(4): 863–83.

Lloyd, G. (1989) 'Woman as other: Sex, gender and subjectivity', *Australian Feminist Studies*, 10: 13–22.

Löfgren, O. (1999) *On Holiday: A History of Vacationing*. Berkeley, CA: University of California Press.

Loker, L. (1993) *The Backpacker Phenomenon II: More Answers to Further Questions*. Townsville: James Cook University of North Queensland.

Loker-Murphy, L. and Pearce, P. (1995) 'Young budget travelers: Backpackers in Australia', *Annals of Tourism Research*, 22(4): 819–43.

Lovell, N. (ed.) (1998) *Locality and Belonging*. London: Routledge.

Lyons, K.D. (2003) 'Ambiguities in volunteer tourism: A case study of Australians participating in a J-1 visitor exchange program', *Tourism Recreation Research*, 28(3): 5–13.

Lyons, K.D. (2005) 'Ambassador, worker and player: Independent travellers working in American summer camps', in B. West (ed.), *Down the Road: Backpacking and Independent Travel*. Perth: API Network. pp. 93–108.

Lyons, K.D. and Wearing. S. (2008) 'Volunteer tourism as alternative tourism: Journeys beyond otherness', in K.D. Lyons and S. Wearing (eds), *Journeys of Discovery in Volunteer Tourism: International Case Study Perspectives*. Wallingford: CAB International. pp. 3–11.

MacCannell, D. (1973) 'Staged authenticity: Arrangements of social space in tourist settings', *The American Journal of Sociology*, 79(3): 589–603.

MacCannell, D. (1976) *The Tourist: A New Theory of the Leisure Class*. London: Macmillan.

MacCannell, D. (1989) *The Tourist: A New Theory of the Leisure Class* (Rev. edn). New York: Schocken Books.

MacCannell, D. (1992) *Empty Meeting Grounds: The Tourist Papers*. London: Routledge.

MacCannell, D. (2001) 'The commodification of culture', in V.L. Smith and M. Brent (eds), *Hosts and Guests Revisited: Tourism Issues of the 21st Century*. New York: Cognizant Communication Corp. pp. 380–90.

Macleod, D. (2004) *Tourism, Globalisation and Cultural Change: An Island Community Perspective*. Clevedon: Channel View Press.

Macleod, D. (2006) 'Cultural commodification and tourism: A very special relationship', *Tourism Culture & Communication*, 6(2): 71–84.

Maoz, D. (2006) 'The mutual gaze', *Annals of Tourism Research*, 33(1): 221–39.

Markwell, K. (2001) 'An intimate rendezvous with nature?: Mediating the tourist–nature experience at three tourist sites in Borneo', *Tourist Studies*, 1(1): 39–57.

Markwell, K. and Basche, C. (1998) 'Using personal diaries to collect data', *Annals of Tourism Research*, 25(1): 228–45.

Markwell, K., Stevenson, D. and Rowe, D. (2004) 'Footsteps and memories: Interpreting landscapes through thematic walking tours', *The International Journal of Heritage Studies*, 10(5): 457–73.

Matthews, A. (2008a) 'Negotiated selves: Exploring the impact of local–global interactions on young volunteer travellers', in K.D. Lyons and S. Wearing (eds), *Journeys of Discovery in Volunteer Tourism: International Case Study Perspectives*. Wallingford: CAB International. pp. 101–17.

Matthews, A. (2008b) 'Backpacking as a contemporary rite of passage: Victor Turner and youth travel practices', in G. St John (ed.), *Victor Turner and Contemporary Cultural Performance*. New York and Oxford: Berghahn.

Matthews, A. (forthcoming) 'Living paradoxically: Understanding the discourse of authentic freedom as it emerges in the travel space', *Tourism and the Media*, special edition, *Tourism Analysis*.

May, J. (1996) 'In search of authenticity off and on the beaten track', *Environment and Planning D: Society and Space*, 14(3): 709–36.

Mbaiwa, J.E. (2004) 'The socio-cultural impacts of tourism development in the Okavango Delta, Botswana', *Journal of Tourism and Cultural Change*, 2(3): 163–84.

McCabe, S. (2005) 'Who is a tourist?: A critical review', *Tourist Studies*, 5(1): 85–106.

McGhee, N.G. and Andereck, K. (2008) 'Pettin the critters: Exploring the complex relationship between volunteers and the voluntoured in McDowell County, West Virginia, USA, and Tijuana, Mexico', in K.D. Lyons and S. Wearing (eds), *Journeys of Discovery in Volunteer Tourism: International Case Study Perspectives*. Wallingford: CAB International. pp. 12–24.

Mead, G.H. (1934) *Mind, Self, Society*. Chicago: University of Chicago Press.

Meethan, K. (2001) *Tourism in Global Society: Place, Culture, Consumption*. Basingstoke: Palgrave.

Meethan, K. (2003) 'Mobile cultures? Hybridity, tourism and cultural change', *Tourism and Cultural change*, 1(1): 11–28.

Meethan, K., Anderson, A. and Miles, S. (eds) (2006) *Tourism Consumption and Representation: Narratives of Place and Self*. Wallingford: CAB International.

Mellor, A. (1991) 'Enterprise and heritage in the dock', in J. Corner and S. Harvey (eds), *Enterprise and Heritage: Crosscurrents of National Culture*. London: Routledge. pp. 93–115.

Meredith, P. (1998) 'Hybridity in the third space: Rethinking bi-cultural politics in Aotearoa/New Zealand', paper presented to Te Oru Rangahau Maori Research and Development Conference, Massey University, New Zealand. Retrieved October 2008 from: http://lianz.waikato.ac.nz/PAPERS/paul/hybridity.pdf

Mies, M. (1993) 'White man's dilemma: His search for what he has destroyed', in M. Mies and V. Shiva (eds), *Ecofeminism*. Melbourne: Spinifex Press. pp. 132–63.

Miller, D. (1994) *Modernity: An Ethnographic Approach*. Oxford: Berg.

Milne, S. and Ateljevic, I. (2001) 'Tourism, economic development and the global–local nexus: Theory embracing complexity', *Tourism Geographies*, 3(4): 369–93.

Mo, C., Dennis, H.R. and Havitz, M.E. (1993) 'Testing an international tourist role typology', *Annals of Tourism Research*, 20(2): 319–35.

Moles, K. (2008) 'A walk in thirdspace: Place, methods and walking', *Sociological Research Online*, 13: 4. Retrieved 15 January 2008 from: http://www.socresonline.org.uk/13/4/2.html

Momsen, J. (1994) 'Tourism, development and gender in the Caribbean', in V. Kinnaird and D. Hall (eds), *Tourism: A Gender Analysis*. Chichester: Wiley. pp. 106–20.

Moorhouse, H.F. (1983) 'American automobiles and workers dreams', *Sociological Review*, 31: 401–26.

Morawski, S. (1994) 'The hopeless game of *Flânerie*', in K. Tester (ed.), *The Flâneur*. London: Routledge. pp. 181–97.

Morgan, N. and Pritchard, A. (1998) *Tourism Promotion and Power: Creating Images, Creating Identities*. Chichester: John Wiley & Sons.

Mowforth, M. and Munt, I. (1998) *Tourism and Sustainability: New Tourism in the Third World*. London: Routledge.

Mowforth, M. and Munt, I. (2003) *Tourism and Sustainability: Development and New Tourism in the Third World*. London and New York: Routledge.

Mugford, S.K. (1987) 'Cocaine users in three cities: A social profile', paper presented at annual SAANZ Conference, July, University of New South Wales.

Munt, I. (1994) 'The "other" postmodern tourism: Culture, travel and the new middle classes', *Theory, Culture and Society*, 11: 101–23.

Nash, D. (1989) 'Tourism as a form of imperialism', in V.L. Smith (ed.), *Hosts and Guests: The Anthropology of Tourism*. Philadelphia, PA: University of Pennsylvania Press. pp. 37–51.

Nash, R. (1967) *Wilderness and the American Mind*. New Haven, CT: Yale University Press.

Nash, R. (1989) *The Rights of Nature: A History of Environmental Ethics*. Madison, WI: University of Wisconsin Press.

Nordenmark, M. (2004) 'Does gender ideology explain differences between countries regarding the involvement of women and men in paid and unpaid work?', *International Journal of Social Welfare*, 13(3): 233–43.

Noy, C. (2004) 'This trip really changed me: Backpackers' narratives of self-change', *Annals of Tourism Research*, 31(1): 78–102.

Palmer, C. (1994) 'Tourism and colonialism: The experience of the Bahamas', *Annals of Tourism Research*, 21(4): 792–811.

Paterson, M. (2006) *Consumption and Everyday Life*. New York: Routledge.

Pearce, P.L. (1982) *The Social Psychology of Tourist Behaviour*. Oxford and New York: Pergamon.

Pearce, P.L. (1990) 'Social impact of tourism', in T. Griffin (ed.), *The Social, Cultural and Environmental Impacts of Tourism*. Sydney: NSW Tourism Commission. pp. 1–39.

Pepper, D. (1984) *The Roots of Modern Environmentalism*. London: Croom Helm.

Pesman, R. (1996) *Duty Free: Australian Women Abroad*. Melbourne: Oxford University Press.

Phipps, P. (1999) 'Tourists, terrorists, death and value', in R. Kaur and J. Hutnyk (eds), *Travel Worlds: Journeys in Contemporary Cultural Politics*. London and New York: Zed Books. pp. 74–93.

Pigram, J. (1992) 'Alternative tourism: Tourism and sustainable resource management', in V. Smith and W. Eadington (eds), *Tourism Alternatives*. Philadelphia, PA: Pennsylvania Press. pp. 76–87.

Plog, S.C. (1987) 'Understanding psychographics in tourism research', in J.R. Brent-Ritchie and C.R. Goeldner (eds), *Travel, Tourism and Hospitality Research: A Handbook for Managers and Researchers*. New York: Wiley.

Polkinghorne, D. (1988) *Narrative Knowing and the Human Sciences*. Albany, NY: State University of New York Press.

Ponting, J., McDonald, M. and Wearing, S.L. (2005) 'De-constructing wonderland: Surfing tourism in the Mentawai Archipelago, Indonesia', *Loisir et Société/Society and Leisure*, 28(1): 141–62.

Poon, A. (1993) *Tourism, Technologies and Competitive Strategies*. Wallingford: CAB International.

Poria, Y. (2006) 'Tourism and spaces of anonymity: An Israeli lesbian woman's travel experience', *Tourism*, 54(1): 33–42.

Pritchard, A. and Morgan, N. (2000) 'Privileging the male gaze: Gendered tourism landscapes', *Annals of Tourism Research*, 27(4): 884–905.

Pritchard, A., Morgan, N.J., Sedgley, D., Khan, E. and Jenkins, A. (2000) 'Sexuality and holiday choices: Conversations with gay and lesbian tourists', *Leisure Studies*, 19(4): 267–82.

Proshansky, H.M. (1973) 'The environmental crisis in human dignity', *Journal of Social Issues*, 29(4): 12–22.

Raymond, E. (2008) 'Make a difference!: The role of sending organizations in volunteer tourism', in K.D. Lyons and S. Wearing (eds), *Journeys of Discovery in Volunteer Tourism: International Case Study Perspectives*. Wallingford: CAB International. pp. 48–60.

Raz, A.E. (1999) *Riding the Black Ship: Japan and Tokyo Disneyland*. Cambridge, MA: Harvard University Press.

Richards, G. and Wilson, J. (2004) 'Drifting towards the global nomad', in G. Richards and J. Wilson (eds), *The Global Nomad: Backpacker Travel in Theory and Practice*. Clevedon: Channel View. pp. 3–13.

Richter, L.K. (1995) 'Exploring the political role of gender in tourism research', in W.F. Theobald (ed.), *Global Tourism: The Next Decade* (2nd edn). Oxford: Heinemann. pp. 146–57.

Riley, P. (1988) 'Road culture of international long-term budget travellers', *Annals of Tourism Research*, 15(3): 313–28.

Ritzer, G. (2000) *The McDonaldization of Society* (New Century Edition). Thousand Oaks, CA: Pine Forge Press.

Ritzer, G. (2006) 'Islands of the living dead: The social geography of McDonaldization', in G. Ritzer (ed.), *McDonaldization: The Reader* (2nd edn). Thousand Oaks, CA: Pine Forge Press. pp. 32–40.

Ritzer, G. (2007) *The Globalization of Nothing* (2nd edn). Thousand Oaks, CA: SAGE.

Ritzer, G. and Liska, A. (1997) '"McDisneyization" and "post-tourism": Complementary perspectives on contemporary tourism', in C. Rojek and J. Urry (eds), *Touring Cultures: Transformations of Travel and Theory*. London and New York: Routledge. pp. 96–111.

Robertson, G., Mash, M., Tickner, L., Bird, J., Curtis, B. and Putnam, T. (eds) (1994) *Traveller's Tales: Narratives of Home and Displacement*. London: Routledge.

Robinson, J. (2006) *Ordinary Cities: Between Modernity and Development*. London and New York: Routledge.

Robinson, M. (1999) 'Cultural conflicts in tourism: Inevitability and inequality', in M. Robinson and P. Boniface (eds), *Tourism and Cultural Conflicts*. Wallingford and New York: CAB International. pp. 1–32.

Robinson, T. (2006) *Work, Leisure and the Environment: The Vicious Circle of Overwork and Over Consumption*. Cheltenham: Edward Elgar.

Rojek, C. (1985) *Capitalism and Leisure Theory*. London: Tavistock.

Rojek, C. (1993) *Ways of Escape: Modern Transformations in Leisure and Travel*. London: Macmillan.

Rojek, C. (1995) *Decentring Leisure: Rethinking Leisure Theory*. London: SAGE.

Rojek, C. (2005) 'An outline of the action approach to leisure studies', *Leisure Studies*, 24(1): 13–25.

Rojek, C., Shaw, S.M. and Veal, A.J. (2006) 'Introduction: Process and content', in C. Rojek, S.M. Shaw and A.J. Veal (eds), *A Handbook of Leisure Studies*. Basingstoke: Palgrave Macmillan. pp. 1–24.

Rojek, C. and Urry, J. (1997) 'Transformations of travel and theory', in C. Rojek and J. Urry (eds), *Touring Cultures: Transformations of Travel and Theory*. London and New York: Routledge. pp. 1–19.

Rolston III, H. (1992) 'Challenges in environmental ethics', in D. Cooper and J. Palmer (eds), *The Environment in Question: Ethics and Global Issues*. London: Routledge. pp. 135–46.

Ross, G.F. (2005) 'Cyber-tourism and social capital: Ethics, trust and sociability', *Tourism Recreation Research*, 30(3): 87–95.

Roudometof, V. and Robertson, R. (1998) 'The space between the boundaries: Globalization and Americanization', in M.F. Epitropoulos and V. Roudometof (eds), *American Culture in Europe: Interdisciplinary Perspectives*. Westport, CT: Praeger. pp. 181–200.

Routledge, P. (1996) 'The third space as critical engagement', *Antipode*, 28(4): 399–419.

Rowe, D. and Stevenson, D. (1994) 'Provincial paradise: Urban tourism and city imaging outside the metropolis', *The Australian and New Zealand Journal of Sociology*, 30(2): 178–93.

Ruhanen, L., Cooper, C. and Fayos-Solá, E. (2008) 'Volunteering tourism knowledge: A case from the United Nations World Tourism Organization', in K.D. Lyons and S. Wearing (eds), *Journeys of Discovery in Volunteer Tourism: International Case Study Perspectives*. Wallingford: CAB International. pp. 25–35.

Russell, A. (2007) 'Anthropology and ecotourism in European wetlands: Bubbles, babies and bathwater', *Tourist Studies*, 7(2): 225–44.

Ryan, C. and Hall, C.M. (2001) *Sex Tourism: Marginal People and Liminalities*. London: Routledge.

Samdahl, D. (1992) 'The effect of gender socialization on labelling experience as "leisure"', paper presented at the SPRE Leisure Research Symposium, Cincinati, Ohio.

Sánchez-Taylor, J. (2000) 'Tourism and "embodied" commodities: Sex tourism in the Caribbean', in S. Clift and S. Carter (eds), *Tourism and Sex: Culture, Commerce and Coercion*. London: Pinter. pp. 41–53.

Sánchez-Taylor, J. (2001) 'Dollars are a girl's best friend? Female tourists' sexual behaviour in the Caribbean', *Sociology*, 35(3): 749–64.

Sartre, J.P. (1948) *Existentialism and Humanism*. Trans. P. Mairet. London: Methuen.

Scherl, L.M. (1988) 'The wilderness experience: Psychological and motivational considerations of a structured experience in a wilderness setting', unpublished PhD dissertation, James Cook University of North Queensland, Townsville, Australia.

Scheyvens, R. (2002) 'Backpacker tourism and third world development', *Annals of Tourism Research*, 29(1): 144–64.

Schor, J. (1991) *The Overworked American: The Unexpected Decline of Leisure*. New York: Basic Books.

Schor, J.B. (1999) *The Overspent American: Upscaling, Downshifting and the New Consumer*. New York: HarperCollins.

Seabrook, J. (2001) *Travels in the Skin Trade: Tourism and the Sex Industry*. London: Imprint.

Selwyn, T. (1996) 'Introduction', in T. Selwyn (ed.), *The Tourist Image: Myths and Myth Making in Tourism*. Chichester: Wiley. pp. 1–32.

Shafer, E. and Mietz, J. (1969) 'Aesthetic and emotional experiences rate high with northeast wilderness hikers', *Environment and Behaviour*, 1: 187–97.

Sharpley, R. (1994) *Tourism, Tourists and Society*. Huntingdon: ELM.

Shaw, S.M. (2006) 'Resistance', in C. Rojek, S.M. Shaw and A.J. Veal (eds), *A Handbook of Leisure Studies*. London: Palgrave Macmillan. pp. 533–45.

Sheller, M. and Urry, J. (2004) 'Places to play, places in play', in M. Sheller and J. Urry (eds), *Tourism Mobilities: Places to Play, Places in Play*. London and New York: Routledge. pp. 1–10.

Shelton, B.A. and Firestone, J. (1989) 'Household labour time and the gender gap in earnings', *Gender and Society*, 3(1): 105–12.

Sherlock, K. (2001) 'Revisiting the concept of hosts and guests', *Tourist Studies*, 1(3): 271–95.

Shields, R. (1994) 'Fancy footwork: Walter Benjamin's notes on *flânerie*', in K. Tester (ed.), *The Flâneur*. London: Routledge. pp. 61–80.

Shinew, K.J., Floyd, M.F. and Parry, D. (2004) 'Understanding the relationship between race and leisure activities and constraints: Exploring an alternative framework', *Leisure Sciences*, 26: 181–99.

Silver, I. (1993) 'Marketing authenticity in third world countries', *Annals of Tourism Research*, 20(2): 302–18.

Simmel, G. (1936) *The Web of Group Affiliations*. Trans. R. Bendix. New York: Free Press.

Simmel, G. (1964) 'The metropolis and mental life', in K.H. Wolff (ed.), *The Sociology of Georg Simmel*. New York: Free Press. pp. 409–24.

Singer, P. (1975) *Animal Liberation: A New Ethics for Our Treatment of Animals*. New York: Random House.

Skultans, V. (1998) *The Testimony of Lives: Narrative and Memory in Post-Soviet Latvia*. London: Routledge.

Smith, M. (2003) *Issues in Cultural Tourism Studies*. London: Routledge.

Smith, V.L. (ed.) (1977) *Hosts and Guests: The Anthropology of Tourism.* Oxford: Blackwell.

Smith, V.L. (1989) 'Introduction', in V.L. Smith (ed.), *Hosts and Guests: The Anthropology of Tourism* (2nd edn). Philadelphia, PA: University of Pennsylvania Press. pp. 1–17.

Smith, V.L. and Brent, M. (eds) (2001) *Hosts and Guests Revisited: Tourism Issues of the 21st Century.* New York, Sydney and Tokyo: Cognizant Communication Corp.

Sofield, T.H.B. (2003) *Empowerment for Sustainable Tourism Development.* Amsterdam and New York: Pergamon.

Soja, E.W. (1996) *Thirdspace: Journeys to Los Angeles and Other Real and Imagined Places.* Malden, MA: Blackwell.

Sontag, S. (1979) *On Photography.* Harmondsworth: Penguin.

Sorkin, M. (ed.) (1992) *Variations on a Theme Park: The New American City and the End of Public Space.* New York: Hill & Wang.

Spencer, R. (2008) 'Lessons from Cuba: A volunteer army of ambassadors', in K.D. Lyons and S. Wearing (eds), *Journeys of Discovery in Volunteer Tourism: International Case Study Perspectives.* Wallingford: CAB International. pp. 36–47.

Stankey, G. and McCool, S. (eds) (1985) *Proceedings: Symposium on Recreation Choice Behaviour.* United States Forest Service General Technical Report INT–184. Ogden, UT: United States Department of Agriculture.

STA Travel (2007) Press Release, 'STA Travel gives college students a "second home" in Second Life'. Retrieved 10 October 2008 from http://www.statravel.com/cps/rde/xchg/us_division_web_live/hs.xsl/8763.htm

Steiner, C.J. and Reisinger, Y. (2006) 'Understanding existential authenticity', *Annals of Tourism Research*, 33(2): 299–318.

Stevenson, D. (1998) *Agendas in Place: Urban and Cultural Planning for Cities and Regions.* Rockhampton, Qld: Rural, Social and Economic Research Centre, Central Queensland University.

Stevenson, D. (2000) *Art and Organisation: Making Australian Cultural Policy.* Brisbane: University of Queensland Press.

Stevenson, D. (2003) *Cities and Urban Cultures.* Maidenhead and Philadelphia, PA: Open University Press.

Suvantola, J. (2002) *Tourists Experience of Place.* Aldershot: Ashgate.

Swarbrooke, J. (1999) *Sustainable Tourism Management.* Wallingford: CAB International.

Swarbrooke, J. and Horner, S. (1999) *Consumer Behaviour in Tourism.* Oxford: Butterworth-Heinemann.

Tarrant, M.A., Manfredo, M.J. and Driver, B.L. (1994) 'Recollections of outdoor recreation experiences: A psychophysiological perspective', *Journal of Leisure Research*, 26(4): 357–71.

Taylor, J.S. (2000) 'Tourism and "embodied" commodities: Sex tourism in the Caribbean', in S. Clift and S. Carter (eds), *Tourism and Sex: Culture, Commerce and Coercion.* London and New York: Cengage Learning EMEA. pp. 41–53.

Taylor, J. (2001) 'Authenticity and sincerity in tourism', *Annals of Tourism Research*, 28(1): 7–26.

Teas, J. (1974) 'I'm studying monkeys: What do you do? Youth and travellers in Nepal', *Kroeber Anthropological Society Papers*, 67/68: 42–54.

Thompson, J.D. (1967) *Organizations in Action: Social Science Basis of Administrative Theory*. New York: McGraw-Hill.

Timothy, D.J. and Ioannides, D. (2002) 'Tour operator hegemony: Dependency and oligopoly in insular destinations', in Y. Apostolopoulos and D.J. Gayle (eds), *Island Tourism and Sustainable Development: Caribbean, Pacific, and Mediterranean Experiences*. Westport, CT: Praeger. pp. 181–98.

Tomlinson, J. (1999) *Globalization and Culture*. Cambridge: Polity Press.

Turner, L. and Ash, J. (1975) *The Golden Hordes: International Tourism and the Pleasure Periphery*. London: Constable.

Turner, V. (ed.) (1982) *Celebration: Studies in Festivity and Ritual*. Washington, DC: Smithsonian Institution Press.

Uriely, N. (2005) 'The tourist experience: Conceptual developments', *Annals of Tourism Research*, 32(1): 199–216.

Uriely, N., Yonay, Y. and Simchai, D. (2002) 'Backpacking experiences: A type and form analysis', *Annals of Tourism Research*, 29(2): 520–38.

Urry, J. (1990) *The Tourist Gaze*. London: SAGE.

Urry, J. (1995) *Consuming Places*. London: Routledge.

Urry, J. (2000) *Sociology Beyond Societies: Mobilities for the Twenty-first Century*. London and New York: Routledge.

Urry, J. (2002) *The Tourist Gaze* (2nd edn). London: SAGE. (First published 1990.)

Urry, J. (2003) 'Social networks, travel and talk', *British Journal of Sociology*, 54(2): 155–75.

Urry, J. (2005) 'The complexities of the global', *Theory, Culture and Society*, 22(5): 235–54.

Urry, J. (2007) *Mobilities*. Cambridge: Polity Press.

van der Duim, R., Peters, K. and Wearing, S. (2005) 'Planning host and guest interactions: Moving beyond the empty meeting ground in African Encounters', *Current Issues in Tourism*, 8(4): 286–305.

van der Poel, H. (2006) 'Sociology and cultural studies', in C. Rojek, S.M. Shaw and A.J. Veal (eds), *A Handbook of Leisure Studies*. London: Palgrave Macmillan. pp. 93–124.

van Egmond, T. (2007) *Understanding Western Tourists in Developing Countries*. Wallingford: CAB International.

Vogt, J. (1976) 'Wandering: Youth and travel behaviour', *Annals of Tourism Research*, 4(2): 74–105.

Wang, N. (1999) 'Rethinking authenticity in tourism experience', *Annals of Tourism Research*, 26(2): 349–70.

Wang, N. (2000) *Tourism and Modernity: A Sociological Analysis*. Oxford: Pergamon.

Wearing, B. (1998) *Leisure and Feminist Theory*. London: SAGE.

Wearing, B. and Wearing, S. (1988) 'All in a day's leisure: Gender and the concept of leisure', *Leisure Studies*, 7: 111–23.

Wearing, B. and Wearing, S. (1996) 'Refocussing the tourist experience: The *flâneur* and the *choraster*', *Leisure Studies*, 15(4): 229–43.

Wearing, B. and Wearing, S. (2001) 'Conceptualising the selves of tourism', *Leisure Studies*, 20(2): 143–59.

Wearing, S. (2001) *Volunteer Tourism: Experiences that Make a Difference*. Wallingford: CAB International.

Wearing, S. (2002) 'Re-centring the self in volunteer tourism', in G. Dann (ed.), *The Tourist as a Metaphor of the Social World*. Wallingford: CAB International. pp. 237–62.

Wearing, S. and Chatterton, P. (2007) 'The practice of community-based tourism: Developing ecotrekking for the Kokoda Track, Papua New Guinea', paper presented at the 17th CAUTHE annual conference, Tourism: Past Achievements, Future Challenges, Manly, Australia.

Wearing, S. and McDonald, M. (2002) 'The development of community-based tourism: Re-thinking the relationship between tour operators and development agents as intermediaries in rural and isolated area communities', *Journal of Sustainable Tourism*, 10(3): 191–206.

Wearing, S. and Neil, J. (1999) *Ecotourism: Impacts, Potentials and Possibilities*. Oxford: Butterworth-Heinemann.

Wearing, S. and Wearing, M. (2006) 'Rereading the subjugating tourist in neoliberalism: Postcolonial otherness and the tourist experience', *Tourism Analysis*, 11(2): 145–63.

Weaver, D.B. (1998) *Ecotourism in the Less Developed World*. Wallingford: CAB International.

Weaver, D.B. (2000) 'Ecotourism in the context of other tourism types', in D.B. Weaver (ed.), *The Encyclopedia of Ecotourism*. Wallingford: CAB International.

Welsch, W. (1999) 'Transculturality: The puzzling form of cultures today', in M. Featherstone and S. Lash (eds), *Spaces of Culture: City, Nation, World*. London: SAGE. pp. 194–213.

West, B. (2006) 'Consuming national themed environments abroad: Australian working holidaymakers and symbolic national identity in "Aussie" theme pubs', *Tourist Studies*, 6(2): 139–55.

Westerhausen, K. and Macbeth, J. (2003) 'Backpackers and empowered local communities: Natural allies in the struggle for sustainability and local control?', *Tourism Geographies*, 5(1): 71–86.

White, N. and White, P. (2007) 'Home and away: Tourists in a connected world', *Annals of Tourism Research*, 34(1): 88–104.

White, N.R. and White, P.B. (2004) 'Travel as transition: Identity and place', *Annals of Tourism Research*, 31(1): 200–18.

Wickens, E. (2002) 'The sacred and the profane: A tourist typology', *Annals of Tourism Research*, 29(3): 834–51.

Williams, C. (1998) 'Introduction', in C. Williams (ed.), *Travel Culture: Essays on What Makes Us Go*. Westport, CT: Praeger. pp. xi–xxiv.

Williams, R. (1961) *The Long Revolution*. London: Penguin.

Wilson, E. (1995) 'The invisible *flâneur*', in S. Watson, and K. Gibson (eds), *Postmodern Cities and Spaces*. Oxford: Blackwell. pp. 59–79.

Wilson, P. (1997) 'Building social capital: A learning agenda for the twenty-first century', *Urban Studies*, 34: 5–6.

Wolff, J. (1985) 'The invisible *flâneuse*: Women and the literature of modernity', *Theory, Culture and Society*, 2: 37–45.

World Tourism Organization (WTO) (2007) *Tourism Highlights: 2007 Edition*. Madrid: World Tourism Organization.

Yiannakis, A. and Gibson, H. (1992) 'Roles tourists play', *Annals of Tourism Research*, 19(2): 287–303.

Young, T. (2005) 'Between a rock and a hard place: Backpackers at Uluru', in B. West (ed.), *Down the Road: Exploring Backpacker and Independent Travel*. Perth: API Network. pp. 33–53.

Young, T. (2008) 'Mediation of volunteer tourism alternatives: Guidebook representations of travel experiences in Aboriginal Australia', in K.D. Lyons and S. Wearing (eds), *Journeys of Discovery in Volunteer Tourism: International Case Study Perspectives*. Wallingford: CAB International. pp. 195–209.

Young, T. (2009a) 'Framing experiences of Aboriginal Australia: Guidebooks in backpacker travel', *Tourism Analysis*, 14(2).

Young, T. (2009b) 'Welcome to Aboriginal Land: The Uluru – Kata Tjuta National Park', in W. Frost and C.M. Hall (eds), *National Parks and Tourism: International Perspectives on Development, Histories and Change*. New York: Routledge. pp. 128–40.

Yudice, G. (1995) 'Civil society, consumption, and government in an age of global restructuring: An introduction', *Social Text*, 14(4): 209–30.

Zukin, S. (1997) *The Culture of Cities*. Oxford: Blackwell.

Index

Research Methods Books from SAGE

Action Research in the Classroom

Vivienne Baumfield, Elaine Hall & Kate Wall

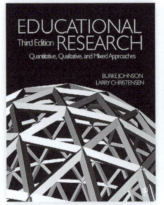

EDUCATIONAL RESEARCH

Third Edition

Quantitative, Qualitative, and Mixed Approaches

BURKE JOHNSON
LARRY CHRISTENSEN

Doing Your EDUCATION RESEARCH PROJECT

Neil Burton
Mark Brundrett
Marion Jones

SECOND EDITION

Action Research

Teachers as Researchers in the Classroom

Craig A. Mertler

Researching with Children & Young People

Research, Design Methods and Analysis

Kay Tisdall, John Davis & Michael Gallagher

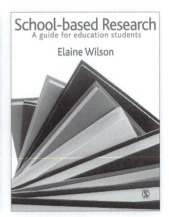

School-based Research

A guide for education students

Elaine Wilson

The Qualitative Research Kit

Edited by Uwe Flick

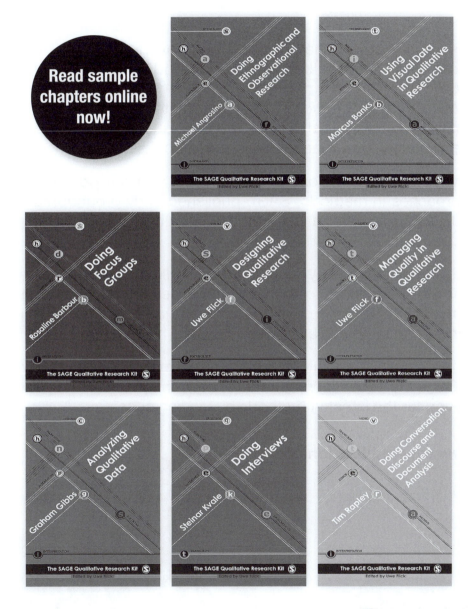

Read sample chapters online now!

Doing Ethnographic and Observational Research — Michael Angrosino

Using Visual Data in Qualitative Research — Marcus Banks

Doing Focus Groups — Rosaline Barbour

Designing Qualitative Research — Uwe Flick

Managing Quality in Qualitative Research — Uwe Flick

Analyzing Qualitative Data — Graham Gibbs

Doing Interviews — Steinar Kvale

Doing Conversation, Discourse and Document Analysis — Tim Rapley

The SAGE Qualitative Research Kit
Edited by Uwe Flick

www.sagepub.co.uk

Supporting researchers for more than forty years

Research methods have always been at the core of SAGE's publishing. Sara Miller McCune founded SAGE in 1965 and soon after, she published SAGE's first methods book, *Public Policy Evaluation*. A few years later, she launched the Quantitative Applications in the Social Sciences series – affectionately known as the 'little green books'.

Always at the forefront of developing and supporting new approaches in methods, SAGE published early groundbreaking texts and journals in the fields of qualitative methods and evaluation.

Today, more than forty years and two million little green books later, SAGE continues to push the boundaries with a growing list of more than 1,200 research methods books, journals, and reference works across the social, behavioural, and health sciences.

From qualitative, quantitative and mixed methods to evaluation, SAGE is the essential resource for academics and practitioners looking for the latest in methods by leading scholars.

www.sagepublications.com